I am
asking
in the
name
of God

Pope Francis

Ten prayers for a future of hope

I am asking in the name of God

First published in the USA in 2023
by Image, an imprint of Random House,
a division of Penguin Random House LLC, New York

First published in Great Britain in 2023

SPCK
SPCK Group
Studio 101
The Record Hall
16–16A Baldwin's Gardens
London EC1N 7RJ

www.spck.org.uk

Book design by Virginia Norey

All Scripture quotations are taken from The New Jerusalem Bible,
copyright © 1985, 1999 by Penguin Random House LLC and Darton,
Longman & Todd, Ltd. Originally published by Darton, Longman & Todd,
Ltd. and Les Editions du Cerf in 1985 and subsequently revised in 1999.
Used by permission. All rights reserved.

British Library Cataloguing-in-Publication Data
A catalogue record for this book is available from the British Library

ISBN 978–0–281–08997–0
eBook ISBN 978–0–281–08999–4

1 3 5 7 9 10 8 6 4 2

First printed in Great Britain by Clays Ltd

eBook by Clays Ltd

Produced on paper from sustainable sources

Certain adjustments to the original Spanish and Italian texts, including colloquialisms, punctuation, and grammar, have been made for the sake of cohesion and consistency.

Note to Readers

✠

I mage Books is honored to publish *I Am Asking in the Name of God: Ten Prayers for a Future of Hope* on the tenth anniversary of Jorge Mario Bergoglio's election as pope, when he took the name of Francis in honor of Saint Francis, the patron saint of the poor. In this book, the pope offers his heartfelt prayers for the world and compelling invitation to us to work together to change our future.

We live in an unprecedented age, never before seen in our lifetime. The pandemic caused by the coronavirus has upended our daily rhythms, our work—our very way of life. More than ever we need books like *I Am Asking in the Name of God* that reconnect us with our faith, restore a hopeful vision for the world, and prioritize our collective holy humanity.

Blessings,
Becky Nesbitt
Editorial Director, Image Books

Contents

Introduction

✝

During my first ten years as pope, you have heard me every week with the same constant petition: "Pray for me." I have said this in audiences, the Angelus, and various speeches. You and your prayers, in the case of believers, and good vibes, from those who do not believe, have accompanied me. They have been a permanent source of energy in my continuing forward with the papacy. For this reason, I would first like to thank you. Second, I would like to tell you that today I place myself in a little more beggarly fashion than usual. I want to share with you ten requests I am making in the name of God to face the future with hope.

I have the same relationship with God as any other person: a very human one. If you read the Bible, you will find characters who sometimes move away from God, hide from God, and fight with God, like when Abraham bargains with him over the righteous of Sodom (see Genesis 18:23–32).

A relationship with God is good when it moves forward along the years, does not remain in its infancy, and is open. It is a bond that matures daily, open to misunderstanding, struggle, and communion that is born every new day. I strive for a relationship like this, even in the dark moments.

I know that God is there, not only when I speak. Sometimes I am merely silent and let God talk so that he will make himself known. It is a relationship of coexistence.

Other times I do not understand God because he has a particular way of proceeding. But, in any case, one thing I am clear on, and it is how God is with me and with all the world: there is a closeness, a way of compassion, and a tenderness. I hope that my relationship may follow this manner.

Sometimes it is formal, such as when I celebrate the sacraments. However, when I enter the formality of the moment, I seek to not be overelaborate—that it would be a formality that is in line with spontaneity. Generally, it is spontaneous and does not consist of talking, talking, and talking. It also involves being in silence and contemplating.

When I was young, it was beneficial for me to read about a saint who was said to spend all his time in the chapel. When asked what he was doing there and how he spoke to God, he responded, "I do not know. God looks at me, and I look at God." Sometimes our relationship with God is like this: wordless. This is an example of a saint. In my case, I do not get to this mystical state, nor even close to it. I must fight for closeness every day.

What I feel for God is love. You cannot love God if you do not feel loved. In life, ingratitude often gets in the way; it is not feeling loved by someone who loves you. Feeling loved is principal in this case.

Today I present to you ten issues that are part of our joint efforts for the sake of the entire human family and to which I would like to offer some proposals. But first, I want to call you so we can all be part of a change process.

As proposed by various analysts, today's world is undergoing a change of epoch rather than an era of change. This diagnosis was given even before the pandemic. We are still suffering from the effects of the pandemic and from the war in Ukraine, which has struck the heart of Europe and had disastrous ramifications across the globe. If there was doubt that humanity is undergoing a hinge moment, the last years have cleared these doubts.

The Church is going through a similar moment because we can no longer think of an institution that is isolated from what is happening around it, whether it be positive or negative changes. As was taught so well to us by the Second Vatican Council Pastoral Constitution *Gaudium et Spes,* if the world is shaken, the Church is shaken with it because the world is the concrete reality in which the Church is rooted. For this reason, these petitions in the name of God are also directed to all God's people.

This change of epoch that we are called to traverse has put in a place of prominence many concerns that, up until recently, did not have the visibility they deserved. I think of, for example, the rejection of all violence against women or the fight against all forms of abuse inside and outside the Church.

And, whether or not we like the changes that the world has undergone in these last years, this is when we are called to move in, and we cannot stand by with our arms folded. Therefore, the first endeavor to advance these ten petitions in the name of God is to accept this reality. The phrase of the Nobel winner in literature, Bertrand Russell, comes to mind: "To understand the actual world as it is, not as we should wish it to be, is the beginning of wisdom."[1]

The world is changing, and we are also invited to birth new changes. This does not mean leaving behind what we have believed and preached our whole lives for a fleeting trend. Instead, it means being prepared so that faith becomes significant and creative in the new context that is to be built. I think, for example, about the transformations brought about by the eruption of telecommunications technology and how it has decidedly changed so many aspects of the daily lives of millions across the globe. Likewise, on the health and bioethical front, incorporating artificial intelligence is a challenge to humanity.

For many people, the world is becoming more unjust and increasingly dangerous due to the wars and global warming that threaten the survival of thousands of species, including our own. Even though we have the advantage that humanity provoked this situation, humans could (and, it is clear, we should) remedy these problems.

Let us think of our brothers and sisters who are migrants and refugees. They are often the concrete and living proof of the disastrous consequences of the problems of the world in which we live. Let us open our hearts to them and extend our open hands to those who have traversed thousands of miles with their families with the sole objective of being a little happier. It is they who are escaping, but any one of us could be in that same situation.

To rectify the various situations brought forth in this book, what I am asking in the name of God requires communal efforts to unite us as the one common family we are. At the same time, it is true that some of the challenges the world has before it can be resolved only if there is a firm and decided involvement by those with more authority. Yet it is clear, whichever may be the case, that if we do not each begin the change at the personal level, we will not arrive at a good destination.

Therefore, I trust the capability of young people to organize, mobilize, and bring about change. For many of the issues about which I ask in the name of God, we must have willing young people who participate in politics that are at the service of a true, universal common good. I remember the beautiful definition penned by an Italian writer who highlighted the fact that young people can "return to politics its lost ethics; they have the possibility to give a different and new meaning to common life."[2]

Let us turn to the example of the defense of our Common Home. While we observe that some countries have only recently awoken from their slumber of material inaction, what do we need to do? It is not only about feeling satisfied with ourselves for recycling our trash or adopting lifestyles that are less aggressive with the Earth. Becoming the change we want to see in the world is the best way to demand that those with significant responsibility adopt the urgent and necessary measures.

I also reflect on the economic issues. Is it right for me to complain about the lack of supplies in hospitals or the quality of highways if when it comes time to pay my taxes I look the other way or find ways around it through tax evasion? The change we desire to see from above must be marked by the path of our own small daily actions.

In the case of many of these issues, we have found greater consensus on diagnosing the current situation. What is now lacking is that we put our hands to work. The poet Rilke wrote a verse that should inspire us in that direction: "The work of the eyes is done. Now go and do the work of the heart with the images captured inside you."*[3]

I ask you to join me in making these ten petitions in the name of God.

---

* Translated from Spanish into English.

I Am Asking in the Name of God

1

In the name of God, I ask that the culture of abuse be eradicated from the Church

✝

I cannot begin without again asking for forgiveness. Our words of repentance will never be enough to console the victims of sexual abuse at the hands of members of the Church. We have deeply sinned: thousands of lives have been ruined by those who were supposed to care for and guide them. What we do will never be enough to try to repair all the damage that we have caused.

We want to look society in the eyes and say that we are committed to combating this evil. We seek a change in the culture that served as the framework for abuse, cover-up, and lack of action for many years. We are making new normative decisions to make available the necessary tools that will help us get to the bottom of this scourge. Considering how little has been done in the past, our commitment to the future can never be too great so that these crimes will not repeat themselves, be covered up, or become entrenched. The absolute responsibility of the Church for the drama of these abuses must be a sincere "never again." It is our duty to sit face-to-face with the victims, their families, and their whole communities and explain the steps we have taken and the changes we are working on. The zero-tolerance policy, which began a few years ago to confront this inhuman phenomenon, must be our north star and guide. We must make the pain of the victims and their families our own, which will serve as an encouragement to reaffirm once more the commitment to guarantee the safety of minors and adults in vulnerable situations.

Merely one case in and of itself is a horror. Let us work so that there are none.

We cannot use as an excuse the fact that "the scourge of the sexual abuse of minors is, and historically has been, a widespread phenomenon in all cultures and societies."[1] The abuse of minors is not only an atrocious crime, but, when committed by a member of the Church, it becomes a wound to God.

Our commitment must be to combat the crimes and prosecute the offenders when they happen. But we must also attend our focus and lend our ear humbly to the victims, open our hearts, and accompany them in the healing process to promote a culture of care beyond the Church's confines.

At the same time, we are aware that the task of combating abuse through the mobilization of greater tools in the legal field will not be enough to go against the crimes if we do not act in an intentional way to prevent them. Thus, prevention must take a central role in this new stage on which we must walk.

There is an educational task that calls us as a society. If abuse is a plague that covers all levels of society, the answer must involve all of us in unison—not only to say "never again" to abuse. From the position of the Church we want to work with all of society in a coordinated fashion and across borders to prevent and combat abuse. The culture of care should go beyond the Church.

People were exposed to damaging experiences because the Church did not do enough to protect minors. As a result, in our buildings, thousands of children were victims of severe crimes under our care. For this reason, we have been moved to acquire knowledge and devise responsible practices, which we will then make available to society in our desire to work together to fight these crimes.

The consequences of the abuse of minors and vulnerable adults last for years. I have referred to this crime as "psychological murder" in that it can cause irreparable harm to the mental health of the victims.[2] Childhood is erased. In the part of life that should be filled with games and learning, instead, there are physical, psychological, and spiritual wounds.

One of the most significant failures, if not the gravest, has been not considering the stories and declarations of the victims. For this reason, in this new stage we are moving toward, we want to give a leading role to the people who have experienced this calvary.

In many cases, the abuse of minors is not reported, especially in a great majority of cases that occur in the family environment. "Rarely, in fact, do victims speak out and seek help. Behind this reluctance there can be shame, confusion, fear of reprisal, various forms of guilt, distrust of institutions, forms of cultural and social conditioning, but also lack of information about services and facilities that can help. Anguish tragically leads to bitterness, even suicide, or at times to seek revenge by doing the same thing."[3]

We need better conditions for all people who have been victims of abuse by members of the Church so that they feel safe to give their testimony. Therefore, it is crucial to generate practices that assure their integrity. We must not create situations that revictimize them but instead must ensure them spiritual and personal accompaniment, whether in judicial procedures or the everyday dimension of their lives.

It is also essential to prepare and form those who are in contact with minors and vulnerable adults to be able to read the unmistakable signs that abuse leaves on many of its victims. The answer is not to wait until the muffled and silenced cry of those who suffer abuse comes to light but rather to be attentive to the thousands of manifestations of desperation and calls for help. In many cases, it was not that individuals did not want to listen; instead, they did not know how to do so. This is something we want to change by training and equipping our institutions.

To accompany those who have been abused is a task that we put as the base of this renewed holistic approach in the fight against these crimes. All those who have a role in their ecclesial community must responsibly advocate for the respect and humane treatment of victims and their families.

"Anyone who welcomes one little child like this in my name welcomes me" (Matthew 18:5). To walk with and listen to the victims is the cornerstone on which we would like to build this new culture of prevention and fight abuse. Part of the work includes respecting the victims' integrity and assuring them that their public lives will not be scrutinized.

With the same focus, we turn our eyes to those accused of these crimes. But, until they are sentenced, we must guarantee a just process to all those implicated, in the sense that the principle of *in dubio pro reo*—innocent until proven guilty—must not be left by the wayside, even in the case of these horrific crimes. Even when the evidence is overwhelming, the testimonies are convincing, or it is evident that the person committed the offense, the right to defense must always be guaranteed.

The Congregation for the Doctrine of the Faith has recommended that complaints of possible abuse not be discounted a priori, even if they are from nonidentified or nonidentifiable persons. The anonymity of the accusation must not lead us to automatically assume the claim is false, though caution must be taken in situations that come in this manner.

The consensus shows that ignoring such accusations simply because they are not signed with a name is harmful. Because of this, it is critical that the person who receives these accusations and indications of possible abuse exercise discernment. We are not to give immediate credit to these claims or deny them absolutely.

We know that the victims need time and space, as well as information on how to make claims. For this reason, we reject a culture of gossip that trivializes the crimes by allowing people to make false claims. This culture is difficult to eradicate within the Church.

The Curia has introduced principles to guide the various normative changes to fight against abuse in all its stages. We know that judicial action is not enough. Instead, we need a holistic approach to work toward this goal, from education to formation, prevention, and the fight against these crimes. But this does not mean that we should not proceed with firmness to apply rigorously canonical legislation foreseen for different situations.

Last year, in the promulgation of the apostolic constitution *Praedicate Evangelium* (Preach the Gospel), the Pontifical Commission for the Protection of Minors was formally instituted as part of the Roman Curia under the work of the Dicastery for the Doctrine of the Faith. The institutionalization of the vital work of this body does not seek to curtail the liberty of action or the thinking of its members; instead, it gives essential focus to creating more comprehensive tools to fight against abuse moving forward into the future.

Recently, we have also reframed the legislative typology from which we position ourselves against this crime. The cases of abuse by members of the clergy were originally considered to fall within the canonical section of "Offences Against Special Obligations"; however, beginning in 2021, in line with the focus on a more holistic approach that we have proposed, it is now designated under "Offences Against Human Life, Dignity and Liberty."[4]

The objective of these reforms that we have embarked on is to have better tools that permit us to judge, prevent, and combat these crimes for the express purpose that within the Church, there would be a respectful and conscious community knowledgeable in the rights and needs of minors and vulnerable people. This reinforces within the whole of the clerical community, members of the institutes of consecrated life, and the laity that we need to consciously grow in our ability to point out signs of abuse before competent authorities.

Since 2019 all members, officials, and employees of the Roman Curia, the diplomatic corps of the Holy See, and all others with an administrative or judicial mandate in the Holy See have had an obligation to present immediate complaints to the promoter of the judicial tribunal of Vatican City whenever, in the exercise of their functions, they have had knowledge or well-founded reasons to believe that a minor or vulnerable person has been the victim of any abuse.

Also, various programs have been put into effect for the sake of training personnel of the Roman Curia and institutions connected to the Holy See on the issues of exploitation, sexual abuses, and the mistreatment of minors and vulnerable people.

In the same spirit, always seeking to approach the fight against abuse from a holistic perspective, with the central axis being the victims and the importance of prevention, the suitability of candidates to interact with minors and vulnerable adults must be verified before hiring any personnel of the Roman Curia and the Vatican.

I repeat: the voices of the victims are the breath of our fight. We know that, since wounds need time to heal, it may take time for these voices to be expressed. For this reason, we have decided to eliminate the twenty-year statute of limitations on cases of abuse. The time for justice must adapt to the victims and not the other way around.

At the same time, these crimes necessitate a quick response

once the claims have been made. Therefore, we cannot allow the destruction of proof or tampering with witnesses. With this objective in mind, we have introduced fines ranging from five thousand euros to six months in jail for people who fail to report accusations of abuse or those who hinder the process unjustifiably.

We will not grow weary in doing everything possible to prevent these crimes and to bring to justice all those who have committed them. We look upon that which has been done in the past with shame, yet we are building a new hermeneutic so that no one will be able to allege a lack of preparation or inexperience. The wound inflicted on all of society by this problem is so great that the battle against it may occupy us permanently.

In the power of prayer, we have the key to acting with discernment, always with the pursuit of justice on the horizon and the desire to avoid postures of grandstanding to compensate for past mistakes and respond to media pressure. We must leave behind these defensive reactionary attitudes that seek to save the institution to the detriment of the victims.

In this sense, already in 2016, we laid out that negligence in cases of abuse was a cause for the dismissal of bishops. That is to say, all serious action destined to muddle or slow down investigations is cause for dismissal. Yet these renewed commitments cannot be made only by the pope, those in charge of the dicasteries, or canonists who reinforce Vatican legislation in the fight against these abuses. We must respond in this way globally and communally against the magnitude of devastation these abuses have caused in many people. As members of the Church, yes, and as members of the broader human family.

There is no structure where actual change has not begun from below and from the inside. Therefore, we are called to walk together to eradicate the culture of abuse from our communities and to start a true ecclesial and social transformation not only as pastors, religious, and consecrated persons but also as laypersons. We need to unify our voices and hands as members of the Church to transform this reality.

Our Church, our mother, calls each of her children to confront this new challenge: "Even today we see how often in families the first reaction is to cover everything up; a first reaction that is still present in other institutions, and in the Church too. We must fight against this old habit of covering up."[5] In our unified fight as those baptized, we must be vigilant to the behaviors of our brothers and sisters. We cannot continue to operate in covering up these abuses.

From pastoral positions to education, all institutions are called to take a step forward. Only by forming a preventative alliance as the whole people of God will we eradicate this culture of death, which is the bearer of all sexual abuse, mental abuse, and abuse of power.

"If one part is hurt, all the parts share its pain" (1 Corinthians 12:26). These words by Saint Paul remind us that we are all called to a permanent mobilization against this plague of abuses.

I remember something I mentioned on my trip to Canada, in meeting with bishops, priests, deacons, consecrated persons, seminarians, and pastoral workers:

> The Church in Canada has set out on a new path, after being hurt and devastated by the evil perpetrated by some of its sons and daughters. I think in particular of the sexual abuse of minors and vulnerable people, scandals that require firm action and an irreversible commitment. Together with you, I would like once more to ask forgiveness of all the victims. The pain and the shame we feel must become an occasion for conversion: never again! And thinking about the process of healing and reconciliation with our indigenous brothers and sisters, never again can the

Christian community allow itself to be infected by the idea that one culture is superior to others, or that it is legitimate to employ ways of coercing others.[6]

The dynamism of the contemporary world obligates us to the work of education and constant prevention. To the past mistakes of sexual abuse, mental abuse, and the abuse of power that the Church has had to confront, we now add new challenges that come at the hand of the eruption of new technologies.

The protection of minors must include new forms of sexual abuse and all forms of abuse that threaten the spaces in which they live and the latest tools they use. The grooming of children, the production and possession of child pornography, and the harassment of minors and vulnerable adults through social media cannot make us indifferent to this challenge.

Brothers and sisters, men and women of goodwill of the entire world: as we face this global evil entrenched in all levels of society, the abuse of minors, it is clear that no single institution can battle against these crimes. It is worth nothing to solely reform the legal framework and increase the penalty for these crimes if there is not also a change in our consciousness that makes us say "never again." Therefore, alongside education, we must continue to work to prevent these crimes. To the victims, to whom our plea for forgiveness is not enough, we give our word to our commitment to continue a zero-tolerance policy. And for all this I ask, in the name of God, that we continue to fight against a culture of sexual abuse, the abuse of power, and that of our minds, which is truly a culture of death.

2

In the name of God,
I ask that we protect our Common Home

+

Our planet is in danger. We have lived the last decades under a voracious system that has not only pushed millions of human beings to the brink of disaster but has also exposed this place to limits before unseen in our Common Home, Mother Earth.

A socioeconomic system based on greed has required even the plundering of nature to sustain the pace of consumption and wastefulness inherent in it. The unbridled consumerism of the few, which has been made possible only by the exclusion of others, and the constant aggression toward nature have run the risk of the Earth being irreparably damaged. In the name of God, I ask that we defend and protect our Common Home. The clock is ticking, and all of life is in danger, yet we still have time. I have made my own the creative protest slogan against this model of depredation: there is no plan(et) B.

I want to ask the large mining corporations, the oil industry, forestry companies, real estate conglomerates, and agribusiness to stop destroying forests, wetlands, and mountains and to cease contaminating rivers and seas and poisoning our people and food.[1] I reiterate the danger laid out in my encyclical letter *Laudato Si'*: "If present trends continue, this century may well witness extraordinary climate change and an unprecedented destruction of ecosystems, with serious consequences for all of us."[2]

Living in peace is also living in harmony with our Earth. It is part of our doctrine: *"Care for the environment represents a challenge for all of humanity. It is a matter of a common and universal duty, that of respecting a common good,* destined for all, by preventing anyone from using 'with impunity the different categories of beings, whether living or inanimate—animals, plants, the natural elements—simply as one wishes, according to one's own economic needs.'"[3]

The evidence of the constant aggressions against our Common Home is already palpable and in danger of becoming irreversible if we do not act immediately. The loss of biodiversity, the degradation of our environment, and global warming are merely some inevitable consequences of our actions since we have already greedily consumed more earthly resources than the planet can continue to support.

This voraciousness toward our natural resources merely to uphold a system of death exemplifies an enormous injustice. It is the poorest who suffer the most extraordinary consequences: those who live in the humblest and most precarious homes close to the coasts, those who depend on crops to nourish themselves or who have difficulty accessing water. At the same time, those living in the most-developed countries abuse our shared resources. The environmental debacle we have helped create should remind us that creation is not a piece of property we can dispose of at every whim. Just the opposite. An important fact to outline for all of the world governments is that creation is not the property of a mere few; it is a marvelous gift that God has given to us to take care of, and we live in it for the benefit of all, always with respect and gratitude.

Defending our Common Home is not merely an environmental concern but a moral imperative.

Some people have voiced concerns about a particular trend of global summits that have been held to discuss the causes and consequences of the deterioration of the Earth yet lack the accompanying concrete and lasting actions that beg for courage from world leaders. Experts wonder how it is possible that the interests of particular groups end up being imposed on states and international organizations, all while continuing their destruction of creation.

I recognize that there have been some advancements in certain areas that must be highlighted. Some European governments, for example, put conditions on economic relief packages to public and private companies, depending on their commitments to and concrete objectives regarding environmental issues, such as reducing emissions. Other executives implement subsidies for the conversion of the power grid, even directing help to homes so that they minimize the use of fossil fuels.

The defense and protection of our Common Home requires courage. There is now a consensus among the scientific community that even by changing our way of life immediately in the most-developed countries, it would take years to return to the state of the Earth's health at the end of the last century, when the situation was already grave.

The Earth precedes us and has been given to us.

It is also in the very Social Doctrine of the Church, which says that humans must not "make arbitrary use of the earth, subjecting it without restraint to his will, as though it did not have its own requisites and a prior God-given purpose, which man can indeed develop but must not betray."[4]

Let us remember that we are mere stewards of the goods of the Earth, even though the current system seeks to confuse stewardship for a culture based on accumulation and seemingly limitless consumption. We are not proprietors of the creation to exploit it for our self-interest and growth.

The moment to act is today, not tomorrow. The consequences are those of the present, not of a distant future. Perhaps it is one of the most urgent challenges humanity presently faces.

We can make a decisive turn to move in the other direction. We can go from a culture of waste to a culture of care: to take care of our Common Home is to care for our whole human family. It is to care for our own selves. We are invited to a true conversion that would lead to a more harmonious lifestyle with our Earth and its species. This conversion requires from us small actions, which we each can take. The change must begin by us at home, as well as by those who occupy positions of great responsibility in the different spheres of society.

We need governments to lead the way in one of the most critical missions humanity faces. We must ask for the earliest adoption of measures that would take bold actions to slow down the average global temperature increase and would reinforce international cooperation with it. Many processes must be put into effect immediately: promoting the transition to clean energy; adopting sustainable practices for the use of our land that preserve forests and biodiversity; favoring food systems that respect the environment and local cultures; continuing the fight against hunger and malnutrition; and supporting lifestyles of sustainable consumption and production. But we also need an enormous commitment to achieve this common goal.

The case of clean energy is a particular example. While the usage of clean energy is, in fact, growing, a meager level of access persists at a global level. It is still necessary to develop suitable technologies that can be made available more equitably to all humanity. It would be advantageous if the most-developed nations' advances in this regard were accompanied by the transfer of knowledge, technology, and resources to the poorest countries for their implementation.

The coronavirus pandemic made clear the interconnected nature of all peoples—an interconnectedness caught between a globalization of indifference and greater global solidarity. This is why it is crucial that the effects of this transition away from a culture of limitless consumption, while both necessary and urgent, do not fall on the weakest, the least-developed nations, or the working class. This environmental conversion should not be an excuse for reducing work opportunities.

This transition should bring us toward a more just, sustainable, and mutual social contract. We need more circular processes that produce and do not waste the resources of our Earth. We must form more fair means for distributing goods and more responsible practices when we consume. We can all be the change we desire if we unite the human family to pursue more sustainable and holistic development. Three words can help us in the task before us: commitment, responsibility, and solidarity.

Our responsibility to the youth is not a mere suggestion; it is required. They have shown, in many cases, to be our teachers on the path to finding a solution to stop the damage to our planet. I see in young people a commitment, creativity, and resilience concerning the environmental issues that their grandparents, like my generation, or their parents did not have. We have sinned, and we repent. We do not merely ask to learn from our past errors; it is necessary to correct them.

For this reason, the youth are needed to mark the path ahead, leading the governments of the world and us. Criticize, then take to the streets, mobilize, but above all, change.

We need a virtuous harmony between the adults' words and the youths' actions. The enthusiasm and commitment of the youth serve as a constant reminder that hope is not a utopia and that peace is always a possible outcome. Among all the wounds we have made to our Common Home, biodiversity loss is one of the most visible and irreversible. The list of species in danger of extinction grows by the day. I am not merely speaking of animals but of whole ecosystems, which are the substratum of life and in many cases play a crucial role in maintaining environmental balance. The conversion we need must include in-depth environmental research and evaluation before putting into place extractive, energy, forestry, or any other industries that destroy and contaminate the most fragile ecosystems in the world. I think of the example of the Amazon, where in many cases, the complicity between state and business, motivated by the avarice of new economic projects, rolls over all life, including human life.

As part of the Catholic Church, we must take steps to introduce into the *Catechism* the sin against the environment, which are ecological sins against our Common Home. I am happy that this initiative has been supported by the Synod of Bishops for the Pan-Amazon Region, who have, in particular, proposed to define ecological sin as an action and omission against God, our neighbor, our community, and the environment.[5]

It was my predecessors who, in the last half century, warned of the rapid deterioration of our Earth and of human inaction. Saint Paul VI, over fifty years ago, already had considered the environmental crisis of his time "a dramatic and unexpected consequence" of unbridled human activity, caused by the "ill-considered exploitation of nature," which "risks destroying it" and causing humanity to become "in his turn the victim of this degradation."[6] In this century, Saint John Paul II called for global environmental conversion, and Benedict XVI asked to "correct models of growth that seem incapable of guaranteeing respect for the environment."[7]

There is something clear: this is a sin against future generations. Those who harm our Earth in this unrestrained and careless manner cannot be considered good Christians. Ecocide is a crime against peace and humanity and must be recognized by the international community.

It is important to remember the historic position of the Social Doctrine of the Church, that *"a correct understanding of the environment prevents the utilitarian reduction of nature to a mere object to be manipulated and exploited. At the same time, it must not absolutize nature and place it above the dignity of the human person himself.* In this latter case, one can go so far as to divinize nature or the earth, as can readily be seen in certain ecological movements that seek to gain an internationally guaranteed institutional status for their beliefs."[8]

One of the points all eyes are on is how to harmonize human activities with respect to our Common Home. We need a consensus that can overcome the antagonistic positions of those who, on the one extreme, "uphold the myth of progress and tell us that ecological problems will solve themselves simply with the application of new technology and without any need for ethical considerations or deep change," and those who, on the other extreme, "view men and women and all their interventions as no more than a threat, jeopardizing the global ecosystem, and consequently the presence of human beings on the planet should be reduced and all forms of intervention prohibited."[9]

Environmental problems are multicausal and have varied consequences; this is why it is necessary to approach them with holistic answers born from the dialogue between various inputs across different disciplines and points of view. For this reason, I renew my call that we should reflect on ways we can identify, always in constructive dialogue, "viable future scenarios . . . , since there is no one path to a solution."[10]

Today there exists a problem of overdiagnosis with few concrete answers. Due to this, I call on, as I did in *Laudato Si'*, a "responsible scientific and social debate . . . , one capable of considering all the available information and of calling things by their name,"[11] that can ignore the political, economic, and ideological motivations that can potentially change the data according to their interests to produce desired outcomes.

In the framework of action, it is fundamental that we find holistic solutions that are not dissociated from natural and social systems. The crisis is singular and socioenvironmental. We shall be better equipped to resolve it if we approach it from a holistic view and not partially, considering, on the one hand, social aspects and, on the other hand, the environmental impact. This is why "strategies for a solution demand an integrated approach to combating poverty, restoring dignity to the excluded, and at the same time protecting nature."[12]

One of the examples that comes to my mind is the philosophy *buen vivir,** which is seen in many indigenous peoples in the areas of the Amazon, although not only there. It is a philosophy that seeks to live in "harmony with oneself, with nature, with human beings and with the supreme being."[13]

This philosophy is a symbol of a respectful relationship with creation, and in many cases, it dates to many centuries ago. The indigenous peoples do not see the Earth as merely an economic good but rather a gift from God and from the ancestors who now lie in it. Land is a sacred place with which they interact to sustain their identity and values. But as I have said elsewhere, we should not confuse it with the *dolce vita*† or the *dolce far niente.*‡[14]

The framework in which we should pay careful attention to the experiences of these indigenous peoples and their bond with Mother Earth is that, amid this complex and profound socioenvi-

---

* Spanish: "live good" or "living well."

† Italian: "the good life."

‡ Italian: "sweet doing nothing" (the desire for the enjoyment of idleness or careless ease).

ronmental crisis, "many intensive forms of environmental exploitation and degradation not only exhaust the resources which
provide local communities with their livelihood, but also undo
the social structures which, for a long time, shaped cultural identity and their sense of the meaning of life and community."[15] We
must protect alternative, nonhegemonic lifestyles that demon-
strate care and respect for creation.

It is necessary to incite and favor implementing programs and
projects that permit indigenous peoples to stay on their land.
Indigenous peoples, with their ancestral knowledge, guarantee
the care of their lands. In this sense, it is not by chance that many
of the extractive projects do not consider the degradation of nature or culture, including using force to evict indigenous peoples
or reject their ancestral traditions. These peoples receive intense
pressure to leave their lands when the greed for the fruits of the
subsoil is dominated by the desires of business.

The conversion we need must be holistic. However, we must
be wary of positions that defend nature but at the same time
promote abortion and the death penalty. If our focus is on the
lives of those around us, on those who are even invisible to us,
how could we not defend life in all its stages?

In the name of God, I ask that we protect our Common Home.
Saint Francis of Assisi, from whom I took my name and the inspiration of my papacy, reminded us almost eight centuries ago
that we must see nature as our sister with whom we share our
existence and as a beautiful mother who holds us in her arms.
We must act now for her, her grandchildren, and the generations
to whom we must pass the baton in the care of creation. I ask
this in the name of God—with the responsibility that this grave
situation demands, but also with the hope that all is not lost.

3

In the name of God, I ask for the media to fight fake news and avoid hate speech

✝

The world of communications has profoundly changed in the last years and has witnessed incredible acceleration in its constant advance. Even the youngest, the "digital natives," are familiar with these permanent changes in how they communicate and relate to one another. Imagine what is happening to us elderly, who grew up in an era in which the radio and newspapers were the only windows to see what was happening outside our communities.

Our ways of relating and informing ourselves are affected by the rhythms of the advance of science and technology. This new paradigm of technology and communication has opened up tremendous opportunities, if we know how to navigate them and take advantage of them, and to better many people's lives in significant ways. But this calls us to be attentive and responsible so that the use of these technologies is always toward the common good.

This is a shared responsibility, from the users all the way to the companies. From the media outlets to the government. Even the Church needs to contribute our part in promoting the responsible use of technology and ways to communicate that benefit humankind.

We are all called to create a culture that fights against fake news, avoids hate speech, and develops a technological framework that takes care of the most vulnerable.

Specifically, I renew my plea that mass media end the logic of post-truth, disinformation, defamation, slander, and the fascination for scandal and, instead, seek to contribute to a culture of dialogue and reflection, with necessary disagreement and confrontation but without the need to denigrate or mistreat others. It is essential that we take steps to stop the growth of hate speech, indoctrination, and political manipulation, which many times take advantage of the fragility and vulnerability of people's social situations. Dialogue and social friendship will result in public policies that can minimize the threat generated by a culture of fake news.

One thought I would like to share with you relates to media outlets. Technological advancement and the configuration of this new paradigm of an overflowing and instant amount of information have reconfigured the role that telecommunications companies play in our society.

The opinions of millions worldwide are formed by the mass media outlets, who have in their hands the indispensable elements to help educate people and stimulate fraternity. Therefore, they are the cornerstone for building society. But, as is true for each of us in our own environment, this role is not exempt from the dangerous desires to manipulate and convert what is meant for good into an instrument to cause harm.

Today, many temptations surround us. One example is slander, which in particular sullies the dignity of others. With frequency, we see news stories that end up being false taking up the front page of newspapers . . . and then the rectifications are merely a tiny line at the bottom of the page.

The slander that circulates in the media can quickly turn into defamation. This occurs especially when people dive into another's past actions with the sole objective of hurting his reputation, even though the person has changed or amended his mistakes. How accurate is Miguel de Cervantes when he discovers these temptations and advises in *Don Quixote de la Mancha* how to alter the written word: "The pen is the tongue of the soul; as are the thoughts engendered there, so will be the things written."[1]

These ideals appear with greater frequency in the political sphere. Political rivalry—including that of "friendly fire"—tempts politicians to rummage through an opponent's past to attack him, no matter the consequences to his family, surroundings, or life. Sadly, many times the media is complicit and plays an active role. In my native country, we call it *carpetazo*,* a carryover from the era of paper archives. Today, we could call it the digital *archivazo*.† This is wrong: it is a sin, it hurts the integrity of people, and it threatens democratic coexistence.

We see the growth of disinformation related to slander, whether it be for self-interest or directed at political power. For this reason, truth must be cared for by and demanded from those being informed. We are obligated to request that we are not misinformed. It would be helpful if the media had greater transparency and always shared who their investors, owners, and advertisers are. This would reveal when there is a conflict of interest at the time of reporting.

We can strive for communication that focuses on positive and constructive stories without falling into complacent goodness. That inquires and investigates yet puts at its center the human person. How many examples of altruism or how many "next-

---

*   Spanish: literally, the slamming of a folder—meaning sharing compromising information about someone.

†   The same idea but in reference to the digital archive.

door saints" do not make the cover of the newspaper? Instead, our attachment to scandal and the negative lead to more coverage of these stories.[2] For this, I reiterate my request that the media does not fall into the trap of seeking to always communicate scandal and ugly things that end up causing much harm.

I think especially of the news in the judicial world, which in my youth we called "police" news. In this media space, caution is crucial in not being alarmist or causing social panic when reporting on crimes.

The presumption of innocence must be respected as a guarantee for information committed to the common good. No one wins when the legal processes are narrated with sensationalized ends, when they immediately convert suspects into culprits, expose the victims' private lives, or encourage people to be "canceled" by the media. Let us not forget that our brothers' and sisters' human life and dignity are at stake here.

No one is born knowing the difference between true and false news, free from the temptations of gossip and sensationalism. We must educate ourselves not to become easily swayed by the attempts to manipulate us in those directions. I invoke the writing of Dostoevsky: "A hundred suspicions will never make a proof."[3]

These temptations can turn media outlets from their formative role toward the dangerous shores of slander, defamation, and "cancellation" of people. And they can border on a more significant institutional crisis when they attempt to undermine the basis of a democratic society.

I refer to lawfare, which many researchers have theorized on and which threatens many of our societies with increasing danger. In Latin America, for example, many dictatorships have begun with the same modus operandi: "diluting media, putting the media in the hands of persons without scruples, of a government without scruples."[4] The sequence is as follows: "Laws exist for media; those laws get canceled. The whole method of communication is given to a company, to a society of slander, that tells falsities, debilitating democratic life. Then it goes to the judges to make judgments on the weakened institution. These people are destroyed, condemned, and then a dictatorship goes forward."[5]

Before judges across the world, I have shown my concern for these types of systems. Judicial processes that put at risk the democracy of nations are generally used to erode emerging political methods and tend toward the systemic violation of social rights. Oftentimes there is evidence of complicity by sectors of the judicial wing alongside the media industry (sometimes known as the "fourth power").

"In civil life, in political life, when there is a desire to launch a coup d'état, the media begins to speak ill of the people, the leaders. With slander and defamation, the media smears the leaders. Later comes the justice system, which condemns the people, and in the end comes the overthrow of the state. It is one of the most corrupt systems."[6]

The Gospel of John reminds us that "the truth will set you free" (8:32). Therefore, the call is to confront all types of false stories. So-called fake news, understood as disinformation spread online or through traditional media, is based on nonexistent or distorted facts, which aim to deceive and even manipulate the reader to achieve a specific objective: influencing political decisions or securing financial gain. We cannot take our gaze away from this growing phenomenon in modern society, which is closely linked to previous problems in many cases, such as that of the so-called cancel culture.

Current events ask us to always be seen, analyzed, and judged with the hermeneutic of the day and not with bygone metrics.

Yet specific current trends border on ideological colonization and seek to reduce freedom of expression. We must raise the banners in defense of the most disadvantaged and those without voice.

In this way, in the name of the defense of diversity, each identity is often erased. This comes with the risk of silencing the positions that defend a respectful and balanced ideal of different sensibilities. It seeks to impose a dangerous sphere-like gaze that counters the richness of the multiculturality of societies in which we live, which is closer to a polyhedron in which different realities can coexist without opposing one another.

Some people want to "project onto the past the history they would like to have now, which requires them to cancel what came before." What is true, however, is that "for there to be true history there must be memory, which demands that we acknowledge the paths already trod, even if they are shameful."[7] We cannot look at our past with partisan eyes or one-eyed gazes. And those who do not know their history are condemned to repeat it.

These trends risk obligating us to deny and rewrite history in terms of contemporary standards. We want to judge previous actions with "Hindsight is 20/20," as it is said in some of our countries.

Another area of concern is the proliferation of hate speech, especially on social media or other news formats that guarantee anonymity. I understand there has been a desire to conserve the Web and its various spaces as a place with the most expansive freedom of speech. Still, the evolution of using the internet as a tool to attack and disqualify others should cause us to reconsider the ways in which as a society we think about and use this space.

What is the point of freedom of speech when we see the growth of "trolls"—users created to multiply the presence of certain content online and to incite and manipulate debates online? While they are extensive on social media, trolls also appear with greater frequency in traditional media, based on those who incessantly comment on published stories online. In addition, many in the press are conscious of the attacks and hate speech that proliferate among those who visit their websites. Therefore, the media restricts or eliminates the publication of specific news stories.

Even still, today humans communicate through and are informed by channels that exceed traditional media. Advances in science and technology make it possible to have a constant communication center in our pockets. We interact with one another with merely a click, we show our opinions with a like, and we can maintain contact with a group of people who live far away or whom we have not seen in a while. But the truth remains that human contact is irreplaceable. We see it at airports and train stations: warm embraces in departures or reunions that remind us that we cannot live alone. During the pandemic, the virtual nature of communication made it possible for us to communicate without being in person, yet we missed the embrace. Children missed the company of their teachers at school, and friends missed the chance to share a table together. Virtual communication will never be able to replace sharing in one another's company. Yes, technology can be an aid, but it will never be able to permanently substitute for relationships and times together.

This new technology has other warnings to it. We need to manage how artificial intelligence becomes part of our lives and not merely be passive observers of the paradigm shifts that will shape us and the generations to come.

If we were more aware of new technologies and their implications, would we pay closer attention to how much we expose our children to them in this digitally globalized world? It is already accepted that at least 25 percent of all internet users are minors and about eight hundred million children get into the digital ship with varying frequency.[8]

What protection can we assure our children so that their discovery of this new world does not jeopardize healthy growth and a peaceful passage through childhood? How are we called to involve ourselves in society as parents, companies, and governments to safeguard our youth from undesirable exposure or, in the worst of cases, potentially dangerous exposure that affects their dignity and health?

The dangers on the internet are intimidation, bullying, and other forms of abuse. The reality of sextortion—extortion based on sexual images—and the abduction of young people for sexual purposes are red flags that should warn us and concern us.

Many of these dangers involve serious crimes, often of transnational systems engaged in the network of human trafficking and other crimes. There is a vast, complex network of men and women involved in the online trafficking of victims and in virtual prostitution. We are all called to the responsibility of diligently fighting this problem. It is never too late to ask all people, public and private institutions, banks, and financial institutions to not be unwilling accomplices in these crimes. International cooperation is crucial in sharing the sites and access to servers, an essential key in combating these dangers that threaten our minors.

Technology companies and internet providers should not be the only ones seen as responsible for the safeguards of the internet. On the contrary, the responsibility is in all our hands. For this reason, I appeal to governments and companies to work together to provide tools to guarantee the safety of those who access the various sites on the internet.

These ideas are not incompatible with the expressions in recent years that recognize connectivity as a human right. The United Nations issued a declaration in 2016 that states that online freedom is a human right, and one that must be protected.

The Church cannot remain distant from the challenges of this new media situation in the world. Therefore, we are invited to step toward this new virtual space that, like all of society, seems unknown and mysterious. This is a Church on the move: to take steps toward understanding the new digital world.

The internet is inhabited by our communities and families. Why not enter their digital world? What is clear is that this does not mean we should broadcast our Mass via TikTok or convert the images of our martyrs for digital circulation. Yet we can find new language for virtual engagement. The "ends of the earth" (Acts 1:8) that the Bible speaks of are now digital. We can begin a new digital mode of mercy, tenderness, and joy that does not forget the least of these.

4

In the name of God, I ask for Politics that works for the common good

I believe in Politics as a tool for transforming the lives of our brothers and sisters. I believe in Politics with a capital *P*, which is a service that seeks to be a guide for people to organize and express themselves. A fraternal Politics built with the people and not just for them. A Politics based on dialogue, never losing sight of the common good, the true and primary objective.

I also know that some write Politics with a lowercase *p*, and it becomes a bad word. Errors, corruption, and the inefficiency of leaders have led to apathy and generalized skepticism from some sectors of society.[1] Varying interest groups end up winning out when Politics retreats and is replaced by skepticism. The consequence of this Political breakdown is that economics, technocracy, and the law lose their legitimacy and are replaced by the law of the strongest. That is why in the name of God, I ask that we build a Politics that works for the common good. This is our aim and what we hope to rehabilitate.

Last year I had the chance to visit Athens, one of the birthplaces of civilization, where humans found in their conscience to be "political animals" as proposed by Aristotle. There, the great classic thinkers together gave birth to the polis.[2] What is left of those first dreams of people who saw this system of organization as a way to work together for the common good?

Since the beginning of the twentieth century, my predecessors have referred to Politics as the "highest form of charity."[3] I also think of it in this way. This definition can be explained as a practice, perceived as a service for the neighbor, which seeks the common good in society. In this short phrase, we can see the reach and limitations, threats and possibilities.

Why service? Because Politics seeks to decenter the "I" and replace it with "us." Individual or party interests should not factor as determining criteria. In this manner, we can recognize that Jesus came to serve and not to be served. It should be—or it should be once more—about sacrifice and surrender.

Why seek the common good? The Social Doctrine of the Church has as an objective to reach "the sum total of social conditions which allow people, either as groups or as individuals, to reach their fulfilment more fully and more easily."[4] *"The common good is the reason that the political authority exists,"* according to the Social Doctrine of the Church.[5] Also, the *Catechism* teaches that "each human community possesses a common good which permits it to be recognized as such; it is in the political community that its most complete realization is found."[6]

For this reason, I return to the encyclical *Fratelli Tutti* to ask myself alongside you, "Yet can our world function without politics? Can there be an effective process of growth towards universal fraternity and social peace without a sound political life?"[7]

Any reflection on Politics cannot forget who its main protagonist is: the people.

I have defined the people as a "mythic" category. Let us not get confused here with "mythological." Mythic in the sense that it transcends the logical and historical categories for explanation or comprehension but can also include them. Mythic in that it is necessary to enter the spirit, culture, heart, work, history, and purpose of the tradition of the people.

The people are made of social, cultural, and personal relationships that shape and move toward a collective project. It is the construction of a shared identity. And this added benefit that the people have makes them the protagonist of Politics. It makes the people the leading actors in the search for a common good through service.

Since attacking democracy is not a marketable action today, efforts have been made to condemn any popularized sayings with any hint of the "people" or its adjective, the "popular." In recent years, there has been a move away from the meaning of this category of the people by pairing it with "populism" or "populist." But, unfortunately, this shift has made it the only prism through which to view any notion of the people in contemporary reality. The discrediting of political adversaries through the binary division of populist/not populist is one of the maladies of contemporary Politics, one from which few countries are exempt.

We cannot treat the people and populism as synonymous. Populism seeks that small group to appropriate popular sentiments for their own aims, even though different nuances are used to understand these movements in each continent. This kind of populism seeks to exclude and concentrate when it does not manipulate and exacerbate conditions. And populists can be those in leadership as well as the parties when they are transformed by an elite that turns its back on the people who helped them achieve their high status. We know of cases of populism in the twentieth century that began with the legitimacy of the ballot boxes and rampantly moved toward totalitarianism. Today we witness with pain the rebirth of those same authoritarian patterns, which not even Europe can feel safe from.

Politics, when not manipulated by one of these trends, encompasses the love of neighbor, leading us to be Good Samaritans in our personal lives. This kind of Politics leads to a collective project that seeks to benefit the least privileged. Politics, when executed toward the search for the common good, transforms voluntarism into organized action. This is why we say it is the highest form of charity.

Here I reiterate, "Individuals can help others in need, when they join together in initiating social processes of fraternity and justice for all [and] enter the 'field of charity at its most vast, namely political charity.' "[8]

This Politics to which we are pointing finds itself threatened nonetheless by various factors. I do not exaggerate when I say that it is immersed in a crisis affecting many societies and threatening to undermine the general well-being.

One of the emblematic examples of this crisis is that many analysts see the noticeable impoverishment of the level of public debate and discourse. It is increasingly hard to find an exchange of ideas accompanied by respect. This climate of "continuous campaigning" that is happening in modern democracies turns politicians into machines who repeat gimmicky slogans without any real interaction with their political adversaries. With formats that increasingly restrict the possibility of developing ideas, the media cheers for the cheapening of public discourse.

A culture of skepticism is not beneficial for the promotion of the virtues of Politics and democracy. This situation does not make for a society that is trying to solve problems that confront it. We see this especially in the alarming rise of economic insecurity and the inability of the employed to pay their bills (a dangerous and rising phenomenon). Here, populism finds a favorable climate for its continued growth.

It does not help that there is an increasing distance between many people and their perception of politicians, whom they see as more preoccupied with caring for their own interests than those of their fellow citizens. For this reason, I call on politicians to work together to rehabilitate Politics in its highest vocation. In an inflamed climate, with Politics discredited and with deteriorating discourse, we risk disrupting dialogue among various groups. In this way, we can see the configuration of one of the most significant problems in our modern society: polarization.

What solution do we have for polarization? Dialogue, dialogue, and more dialogue. Dialogue to know one another. If I do not know them, I cannot understand them. If I do not understand them, I cannot see what they have to contribute to the dialogue. In contemporary Politics, it often seems like segmented monologues of people speaking individually to a camera rather than conversing among themselves. There is nothing further from debate than this.

The holy Paul VI dedicated his encyclical *Ecclesiam Suam* to the issue of dialogue. There he proposed four conditions for discussion so that it changes into an art "to bring together the union of truth with charity, that of intelligence with love."[9]

In this fashion, the four conditions for genuine dialogue are (1) "clarity before all else," the interchange of thought; (2) "meekness" since it is "peaceful, has no use for extreme methods, is patient under contradiction and inclines towards generosity"; (3) "confidence" in the mere word and that of its interlocutor; (4) and "the prudence of a teacher" that has in mind the conditions of the person who hears, whether psychological or moral.[10] In how many exchanges of Politics can we recognize these characteristics?

Where there is a lack of dialogue, there is division. We see it in the world around us, especially in Politics. Let's take the example of a couple. What happens when they do not speak after a fight and go to sleep? Each one of them is closed off in his or her own world. It is a cold war in the morning.

Now let us bring up the present image of Politics in its lack of dialogue. If I speak to those around me only to convince myself, if I discard the ideas of others, if I deny them and never accept their position as something to learn from, and if I see in the other an enemy, I will contribute to an aggressive social climate that our society is cultivating based on populist rhetoric: increasing radical proposals and spurring on discontent, which, on many occasions, is motivated by legitimate widespread dissatisfaction.

This current climate of aggressiveness is magnified by the spread and usage of mobile technology, in which anonymity has already reached beyond the barrier of that which is unspeakable in public discourse. It is even more problematic when political authorities, without shame, express their positions with aggressive terms toward one another. In the Church, we are not distant from this problem: there is a desire among us to divide based on the categories of "right and left" or "progressive and conservative." Therefore, we must develop solutions to fight against this type of rhetoric.

More than two years ago, I warned members of the accredited diplomatic body of the Holy See that "greater polarization does not help to resolve the real and pressing problems of citizens, especially those who are poorest and most vulnerable, nor can violence, which for no reason can be employed as a means of dealing with political and social issues."[11]

The wound most evident from the lack of dialogue and the defeat of Politics is war. It is the evidence of that which has lost the vocation of unity. Therefore, we need to help promote good Politics that works for the common good, based on dialogue, to transform us into the antidote to polarization.

There are dialogues that Politics must promote as a legitimate tool for building our collective dreams.

More than dialogue, there is a way to build together. Much of the apathy and skepticism generated by Politics is based on the perception of a growing distance between the political leadership and what happens in the lives of people.

Politics, to build fraternity, must work, live, and grow together *with* those most in need, not only *for* them. There is no genuine lasting change if it does not come from the inside and from the ground up. Instead, we see in different situations, from various ideologies, people with good intentions who try to help the poor but do not manage to convey empathy, trust, and support since they are seen as strangers.

I do not want to say that this help does not promote ease; on many occasions, it is the only source of income and food for these people. But if Politics does not overcome its challenges and prejudices to achieve an attitude of closeness, it will be difficult to understand the cultural characteristics of the poor, which are concrete and many times different from those taught in academia or conveyed in idealistic speeches.

It is important to remember that "where the poor are concerned, it is not talk that matters; what matters is rolling up our sleeves and putting our faith into practice through a direct involvement, one that cannot be delegated. At times, however, a kind of laxity can creep in and lead to inconsistent behaviour, including indifference about the poor. . . . It is not a question, then, of approaching the poor with a 'welfare mentality,' as often happens, but of ensuring that no one lacks what is necessary."[12]

Here I trace a line laid out by my predecessors. This good Politics, which I am asking for, is embodied by those most in need. Leo XIII called this "friendship," Pius XI named it "social charity," and Paul VI, with a broader understanding, called it a "civilization of love."[13]

One good example is the work of the Popular Movements, where "collective Samaritans" do not seek to merely adopt an idea outside their people's reality but instead see and analyze concerns and act alongside the people because *they* are the people now organized.[14]

Looking into the eyes of the people will allow Politics and its leadership to establish genuine contact with those most in need, not merely to be reduced to efforts leading up to elections.[15] In this way, those in Politics can walk alongside the people and take stock of their actual needs.

Recent situations, such as the protests in the United States after the murder of George Floyd, are evidence of this: multitudes of people saw this injustice and took a stand. A movement was born and pushed from below. Later, people added to the movement from different perspectives, without trying to appropriate it. A few years ago, I received a visit from professional basketball players from the United States who were moved by these protests, and they brought me a shirt that they had worn to commemorate them. They did Politics with a capital P, working side by side with communities and calling for strikes in their sport to bring awareness to the phenomenon with the motto Black Lives Matter.

Another aspect of this Politics is not neglecting, but promoting, youth participation. If Politics seeks to make the people's dreams a reality, it must involve those who represent their future. I tell young people to get involved in Politics. In *The Divine Comedy,* the poet Dante assigns to the lazy—that is to say, those who remain inactive and neutral—one of the harshest of judgments: he affirms that "both justice and compassion must disdain them."[16] In a climate in which Politics is discredited, young people who share their perspectives in new ways to mobilize leaders are a breath of fresh air. It is young people who have the energy and courage to go beyond that which is socially correct. We do not speak of young people who seem like sheets: starched, ironed, and ready to be put away in the drawers of comfort. No!

We hope for young people who are committed to one another and desire to shake up the system to make space for themselves.

It is a disappointment when Politics distances itself from its people and makes young people feel trapped between apathy and skepticism. It is a grave sin that politicians induce a sense of distrust in young people, pushing them away from the possibility of participating in projects for their future.

During my tenure as archbishop of Buenos Aires, with the help of many collaborators, we put forth two initiatives that aimed to stir up the political bug in high school students in the city. We were trying to reach students in the last stretch of their studies, between the ages of sixteen and seventeen.

With one of those initiatives, the Sister School program, we promoted a system of horizontal solidarity between students in the country's interior and students in the nation's capital, who had greater economic power. We created networks of friends through the exchange of materials and school supplies and through their dreams and common projects, which still endure today. These projects resulted from a culture of encounter, which makes us better at recognizing others as our brothers and sisters.

Through another initiative, the School of Neighbors, students learned about and became interested in the concrete problems around them, such as in their city block, neighborhood, and school. They promoted these projects and encouraged them to be passed as laws in the city's municipal government. This is how many of the "youth laws" came to be, including the proposal to name Buenos Aires a "city of education" in 2006; the "law of sizes" in 2009, which makes the textile industry offer clothing in at least eight different sizes; and the implementation of "healthy kiosks" in 2010, which tried to promote the availability of healthier foods and drinks. The program is still running and has involved over ten thousand students in the city.

The School of Neighbors and the Sister School program were

the foundation for what is now a global private association of the faithful, *Scholas Occurrentes*.

Like soccer, art, and dance, Politics must have its own feeder system to stimulate young people to develop their vocation and participate. We need young people with the "courage to dare" that Dostoevsky writes of.[17] For this reason, I ask that we rehabilitate Politics, leading to greater participation of young people. Distrust in Politics comes when we confuse it for a business, when we think about benefits, such as "What do I get?"

Why does Politics end up being seen as a business? It is due to an evil that is found around the world: corruption. For this reason, I ask politicians to remember the words of a Latin American ex-president: "If you like money, do not get into politics."*

Corruption, unlike sin, is a difficult thing to turn around. Drugged by money or power, corrupt officials become accustomed to breathing in a different atmosphere, that of foul air. They forget what the fresh air of the spirit and its horizons smell like. They are anesthetized, and corruption becomes their natural habitat. This is not a warning solely for corruption as we usually think of it but also for other minor forms of corruption, which are increasingly frequent and, unfortunately, more accepted.

Clearly, corruption is not only in Politics but is also rampant in all of society: we see it in the Church, social organizations, the judicial system, and business. In those sectors, it must be denounced and penalized.

It is equally clear that those who say they are committed to the "highest form of charity" are called to show an extra level of honesty and commitment to transparency, which each member of society has. We are not speaking of supermen or superwomen

* José Alberto "Pepe" Mujica, former president of Uruguay.

but simply asking for the bar to be raised by those in leadership who dedicate themselves to this service.

Being attracted to wealth, first-class flights, and mansions is not illegal. However, I call on those in Politics to live daily with a strong sense of austerity and humility. This sobriety will lessen the temptation of corruption and act as a firm example moving forward. The example of austerity could mobilize more goodwill in others than a thousand party functions.

When leaders distance themselves from the life the majority of their constituents lead, they not only slip into various forms of corruption but also lose the anchor of daily contact with the people who have entrusted them to lead.

This helps us understand why so many nations suffer from an ongoing reality in which their political institutions are discredited. Political leadership must place the common good before any self-interests by serving the people and not using the people. For example, in the Church, we try to find pastors who smell like sheep because they are among their flocks. The current political climate is thirsty for politicians who walk among the people. In this way, we will be able to build a system of doing Politics that seeks the common good and promotes youth participation. This kind of Politics, with these characteristics, is the only antidote to corruption, polarization, and war. This is what I ask for in the name of God.

5

In the name of God, I ask that we stop the madness of war

✝

Over two thousand years ago, the poet Virgil wrote in his verses that there is "no salvation in war."[1] It is hard to believe that since then, the world has not learned the lessons of the barbarism that ensues in the battle between brothers, compatriots, and nations. War is the clearest sign of inhumanity.

The desperate plea to stop war is still present today. For years we have listened to the voices of men and women worried about how to stop all types of armed conflicts. The Magisterium of the Church has not been shy in its condemnation of the cruelty of war. During the nineteenth and twentieth centuries, my predecessors described war as a "scourge" that never helps solve the problems between nations. They talked of it as an "unnecessary massacre" to which "everything may be lost" and, in a definitive stance, proclaimed it "always a defeat for humanity."[2] Today, I ask in the name of God to stop the cruel madness of war. I consider the persistence of conflict among us a true political failure.

Take, for example, the war in Ukraine. The cruel reality of this humanitarian crisis is on the minds of millions of people worldwide. For a long time now, we have witnessed these crises simultaneously in several countries, and they have shown us the cruelty of the horror of war.

During a span of thirty years in the twentieth century, humanity fell twice with the tragedy of world wars. Some still bear on their bodies the horrors of fratricidal madness. For many nations, it took decades to recuperate from the economic and social devastation of these wars. Today we are witnessing fragments of a third world war, and these hostilities threaten to grow to become a global conflict. I make the desperate pleas of Pius XII my own now: "We cannot permit that the tragedy of the world war, with its economic and social ruins, moral aberrations and perturbations fall on humanity for a third time."[3]

The situations of the first two decades of this century have explicitly rejected the wisdom of my predecessors, so I am obligated to add, without any ambiguity, that in no case can a war be considered just. There is no place for the barbarism of war, much less when wars, as in the case of the supposed preventive war, perpetuate an even more unjust position. Recent history has given us examples of manipulated wars, in which pretexts were given and evidence was manipulated to justify the attack on other nations. For this reason, I ask political leaders to stop the curse of war and not manipulate information. I ask that they do not trick their countries into pursuing bellicose goals.

War can never be justified. War can never be a solution. We need only to think of the destructive power of modern weapons and see the devastation that they unleash; many times the situation is left a thousand times worse than before the war began. War does not solve problems but creates and leaves destruction in its wake.

War is also an ineffective answer, for it never resolves the problems it is pretending to solve. Consider Yemen, Libya, and Syria, to name a few examples. Are they better now than they were before the war?

If some believe that war can be the answer, it must be because they are asking for the wrong answers. Today, we witness armed conflicts, invasions, and surprise attacks among nations, which shows that we lack collective memory. Has not the twentieth century taught us the risk that the human family faces every time there is a warlike escalation?

If indeed we are all committed to ending armed conflicts, we need to keep the memories alive that guide us to act in a timely fashion and stop conflicts in their gestation before they intensify into a total military conflict. In order to do so, we need dialogue, negotiation, and the ability to listen with diplomatic creativity and with a political vision to build a future system in which our coexistence is not based on the power of weapons and deterrence.

Because "war is not a ghost from the past but a constant threat,"[4] I want to remind us of what the writer Elie Wiesel, a survivor of the Nazi death camps, would say: that it is vital to undergo a "transfusion of memory."[5] This is a reminder to step back from our present situation to listen to the voices of the past.

Let us listen to those voices so we never have to see the face of war again. This madness leaves a lasting mark on those who suffer war firsthand: let us think of the faces of each mother and child who must flee in desperation, each family outraged, each person cataloged as the collateral damage of attacks that take no account of and have no respect for life.

I see a contradiction among those who revindicate their own Christian roots and then push for armed conflicts to resolve the interests of different parties. No! A good politician must always gamble for peace, and a good Christian must always choose the path of dialogue. If we go to war, it is because of the failure of Politics. Each battle begins with a failure in humanity.

This is why we must redouble our efforts in working toward lasting peace. We will use memory, truth, and justice. We all should be part of the process for the development of peace. It begins in each of our communities and is raised as a demand to our local, national, and world leaders. It is in their hands to take the necessary actions to stop the wars.

To them, in my plea in the name of God, I also ask that we end the production and international distribution of weapons. The world's expanse of weapons is one of the biggest moral scandals of our age. It also shows the contradiction that exists in those who speak of peace and at the same time promote and allow the trade of weapons.

How much more immoral is it that the so-called developed nations often close the doors to those fleeing from wars that they themselves promoted with the sale of weapons. This happens here in Europe, and it is a betrayal of the spirit of our founding fathers.

The arms race proves the amnesia that we suffer from. Worse yet, it is an act of insensitivity. In 2021, amid the global pandemic, military spending increased. Data from an investigation center in Stockholm shows an active increase in the expenditure of dollars destined for weapons.[6]

In wars, millions lose everything, but some gain millions. It is even more bleak to suspect that many modern wars are instigated deliberately. This must stop. To all those in world leadership, I ask in the name of God for a firm commitment that they would end the traffic of weapons that has resulted in so many innocent victims. That they would have the courage and creativity to replace the production of weapons with industries that promote fraternity, the universal common good, and the holistic development of all people.

We need to be reminded that before the current arms trade, small acts of resistance, though isolated, were made by those who have a genuine desire for humanity to be free of wars. A few years ago, in the Italian port of Genoa, the port workers refused to leave ships destined to bring weapons to Yemen, out of concern for the children who would be massacred in that nation.

What a difference, no? The political and legal system had no safeguards to prohibit them traveling to Yemen, despite knowing the destination and intention of those weapons.

Beyond the problem of the trade of international weapons destined for war and armed conflicts is the growing use, in many nations, of those weapons designated for personal use. These are often low-caliber weapons but can even be assault rifles and other firearms of great force. How many cases have we seen of children killed from using them at home? How many massacres have been perpetrated because of the easy access to weapons in some nations?

Whether legal or illegal, whether on a large scale or in local retail, weapons traffic is a severe problem that extends across the world. It would be beneficial if these debates would have greater visibility and if a consensus would be reached at a global level regarding the restriction of the production, commercialization, and ownership of these instruments of death.

When we speak of peace and security on a global level, the first organization that comes to mind is the United Nations (UN), specifically the Security Council. The war in Ukraine is evidence, once more, of the need to design multilateral exchanges that are more agile and effective in resolving conflicts. In moments of war, it is vital to have quicker and better multilateralism.

The UN was created based on a charter that sought to solidify the rejection of the horrors that humanity faced during the two world wars of the twentieth century. But unfortunately, though the threat of atrocities continues to grow, the contemporary world is not in the same place. For this reason, it is necessary to rethink institutions that can respond to the new reality and bear fruit in a way that is supported by the largest group possible.

These are the same ideas I proposed seven years ago during my visit to the UN General Assembly when I stated that "reform and adaptation to the times is always necessary in the pursuit of the ultimate goal of granting all countries, without exception, a share in, and a genuine and equitable influence on, decision-making processes."[7]

The need for these reforms was made even more apparent during the pandemic when the limits facing our current multilateral system were evident. The distribution of vaccines gave us a clear example of how sometimes laws outweigh the most robust sense of solidarity.

We have before us an opportunity we cannot waste! We have the chance to devise and realize those organic reforms in order for the UN to recover its important vocation of serving the human family. The UN needs to return to its vision of taking care of our Common Home, preserving the lives of all people, and promoting peace. Following my predecessor Pope John XXIII, who dedicated a section of his encyclical *Pacem in Terris* to the UN, I promoted in my own encyclical *Fratelli Tutti* the necessary reform "so that the concept of the family of nations can acquire real teeth."[8]

I do not want to attack these organizations, which are in many ways nothing more than the place for nations to meet, for how they determine their politics and activities. Here is an example of the delegitimization and deterioration of this international organism: nations have lost the capacity to listen to one another in mutuality so that decisions are made with consensus and toward the universal common good. The legal infrastructure will all be in vain if there is a lack of commitment among those in discussion, loyal and sincere availability, and the will to accept inevitable concessions born out of the dialogue between partners. If the countries that make up this organization do not show political intention to make these changes work, we will be in a place of regression.

Instead, we see international organizations and nations that impose their ideas or interests without the consultation of local entities. The extreme of this behavior is war, but more temperate situations often lead up to it. I have warned before of "ideological colonization," not only of powerful nations over weaker ones but also of a colonization of nations with vast resources over international organizations.

On my trip to Kazakhstan in September last year, I proposed that "the need . . . to promote dialogue and encounter thus becomes all the more pressing, since nowadays the problem of one is the problem of all, and those who hold greater power in the world have greater responsibility with regard to others, especially those countries most prone to unrest and conflict."[9]

Only if we take advantage of this postpandemic moment to reformulate these organizations can we create institutions that can address these increasingly urgent and significant challenges, such as climate change or the peaceful use of nuclear energy.

In this manner, as I speak in my encyclical letter *Laudato Si'* of promoting an "integral ecology,"[10] I believe that restructuring international organizations must go hand in hand with holistic security. This is not linked to the pursuit of armaments or military force. Instead, in a world with such a level of interconnectivity as the current one, it is impossible to have proper food security without environmental, health, economic, or social security. This hermeneutic needs to be the base of all global institutions we seek to redesign, always appealing toward dialogue, building trust among nations, and encouraging intercultural and multicultural respect.

In this way, "now is the time to stop intensifying rivalries and reinforcing opposing blocs. We need leaders who, on the international level, can enable peoples to grow in mutual understanding and dialogue, and thus give birth to a new 'spirit of Helsinki,' the determination to strengthen multilateralism, to build a more stable and peaceful world, with an eye to future generations."[11]

With this urgency, in the hope of condemning the madness of war and spurring a new international framework for relationships between nations, we can avoid the sword of Damocles, which weighs heavy over humanity in the form of weapons of mass destruction, such as nuclear weapons.

I want to insist on this point. The destructive capacity in our current situation is such that "never has humanity had such power over itself, yet nothing ensures that it will be used wisely, particularly when we consider how it is currently being used. We need but think of the nuclear bombs dropped in the middle of the twentieth century, or the array of technology which Nazism, Communism and other totalitarian regimes have employed to kill millions of people, to say nothing of the increasingly deadly arsenal of weapons available for modern warfare."[12]

In the midst of this shocking scenario, we ask ourselves, who has these nuclear weapons? What controls are there on these weapons? How do we stop the logic that insists on the amassing of nuclear warheads for deterrence?

I have already stated, "We cannot claim to maintain stability in the world through the fear of annihilation, in a volatile situation, suspended on the brink of a nuclear abyss and enclosed behind walls of indifference. As a result, social and economic decisions are being made that lead to tragic situations where human beings and creation itself are discarded rather than protected and preserved."[13]

In this context, I maintain Saint Paul VI's condemnation of this type of armament, which after over half a century is still current: "Arms, and especially the terrible arms that modern science has provided you, engender bad dreams, feed evil sentiments, create nightmares, hostilities, and dark resolutions even before they cause any victims and ruins. They call for enormous expenses. They interrupt projects of solidarity and of useful labor. They warp the outlook of nations."[14]

We should not be condemned to the fear of atomic destruction. We can find paths that are not resolved toward imminent nuclear catastrophe caused by the desire of a few people. It is possible to forge a world without nuclear weapons since we have the will and the available tools. It is a necessary goal, given the threat that this type of weapon poses to the survival of humanity.

In Japan, when I visited this land that had been wounded by atomic madness, I said, "Peace and international stability are incompatible with attempts to build upon the fear of mutual destruction or the threat of total annihilation."[15] The existence of nuclear and atomic weapons puts at risk the continuity of human life on Earth. For this, I ask in the name of God that we stop the madness of war, and work toward a planet that has eradicated weapons. The Reverend Martin Luther King, Jr., a true source of inspiration due to his proclamations for peace, clearly stated during his last speech before being assassinated, "The choice today is no longer between violence and nonviolence. It is either nonviolence or nonexistence."[16] It is our choice.

6

In the name of God, I ask that the doors be opened to immigrants and refugees

✝

"I was hungry and you gave me food, I was thirsty and you gave me drink, I was a stranger and you made me welcome, lacking clothes and you clothed me, sick and you visited me, in prison and you came to see me" (Matthew 25:35–36). These words of Jesus remind us of the drama that thousands of our brothers and sisters suffer daily, hoping to find better living conditions for themselves and their families. It is often not the desire to find a better future, but simply a future, since staying in their nations could guarantee death.

I say this to the immigrants and refugees: I have never forgotten about you. I have held you in my heart since my first trip as the bishop of Rome, on my journey to Lampedusa in 2013. You have always been in my prayers and in my mind. I ask in the name of God that the doors be opened for you. That you be welcomed, protected, integrated, and helped. That you not suffer discrimination. That conditions be improved so that no one has to feel the devastation of leaving his homeland because of political, ethnic, economic, or environmental conflict.

The crisis generated by the coronavirus pandemic, which seems to still be afflicting many nations, shifted our focus to one of the major international humanitarian crises facing our present world.

The multiplication of migrants and humanitarian emergencies has resulted in the displacement of thousands of brothers and sisters who are presently fighting the danger of becoming invisible. It seems paradoxical that while more people seek to emigrate from all five continents, less time and space is dedicated to this crisis on social media or as part of the agenda of most nations. We seem to be anesthetized by this tragedy. Today, the emigration that appears to affect all continents is not limited to just a specific area. Instead, it is becoming a dramatic global issue. Above and beyond the thousands of migrants who move between nations, we see day by day, and even more evident with the pandemic, the increasing number of internally displaced peoples who need to migrate even within their own nation.

It is not just people seeking a decent job or better living conditions. It is men, women, the elderly, and children who are forced to leave their homes with the hope of finding other places of safety, peace, and security.

Jesus is present with each and every one of those people fleeing to save themselves, just as in the times of Herod. Because they are persons and not solely numbers or statistics, we are called to see in them the face of Christ. We are called to action by the faces of the hungry, thirsty, naked, sick, foreign, and incarcerated (see Matthew 25:31–46).

It is in the name of God that I plead for them: "Love the stranger then, for you were once strangers in Egypt" (Deuteronomy 10:19). They are our brothers and sisters who seek a better life away from poverty, hunger, exploitation, and the unjust distribution of resources on our planet. The deterioration of our environment, which is felt more and more, and the war in Ukraine have only made this crisis more evident.

The phenomenon of forced migration, amid the increasing inhumane situations, is a humanitarian crisis that faces all of us. It is not only that we should be concerned about them, as the pandemic showed us, but also that we are all in the same boat. There is in us something that unites us. I am reminded of what I said on the island of Lesbos, a symbol of modern immigration: "The future of us all is at stake, and that future will be peaceful only if it is integrated."[1]

We must come out of the anesthesia that leads us to merely lament the humanitarian tragedies stemming from migration, since it paralyzes us at present to make substantial changes.

I want to invite these four verbs to echo toward all immigrants: welcomed, protected, helped, and integrated. These four verbs can serve as a guide toward a Politics that is fraternal and full of solidarity toward migrants. At the same time, they serve as a map for our relationship with all inhabitants of outlying places, that they must be welcomed, protected, helped, and integrated.

To welcome is to open the door. This requires each nation to honestly assess how many people they are willing to accommodate and to simplify the processes of immigration, which many times are fraught with bureaucratic and economic hurdles for migrants and refugees. An easing of procedures would allow migrants and refugees to safely and legally enter their new country. Welcoming means opening our hearts.

Migrants move from one city to another, from one region to another, from one nation to another, traversing through many countries, fording rivers, scaling mountains, and moving from one continent to the next. International cooperation is essential to create a process of welcoming these migrants that puts the human being at the center of its policies.

There are many ways this can be achieved. If only we could make it possible for migrants and refugees to have the same freedom in which commercial goods are moved around. How can weapons—these instruments of death and destruction—have fewer restrictions to enter and leave nations than women, men, and children who dream of a better future?

Global political leadership must use the tools necessary to promote a new way to welcome them without falling into discrimination that ends up creating first-class and second-class migrants. Why not unite our efforts and commitment to increase and simplify the granting of visas for humanitarian goals or the reuniting of families? What resistance do we need to overcome in the most-developed nations to implement a Politics of hospitality like that which was established with great effort in countries like Lebanon and Bangladesh?

At the same time, if the world does not improve the conditions that lead to massive forced migrations, the decision to limit the quota for secure and legal entry for those who flee war and poverty cannot be deemed anything but hypocritical. It is necessary to stop the high number of deportations that puts the lives of so many at serious risk. We need international legislation that can aptly address these realities.

If the networks of traffickers did not insist on the continued wealth of their business—many times with the complicity of the authorities, including those in the nations they are migrating to—many people would not find themselves tempted to embark on these long and treacherous journeys.

Migrants have so much to offer us. To welcome them is to come out to meet them. This is an action that enriches the whole world in which we live. Going out to meet another can have a positive impact on our own stories. I remember a portion of a poem that proposes:

Touch the hand of a stranger
on a day of stone and pain

and that that hand have the firmness
that that of a friend never had.[2]

Not only do we need to welcome migrants, but we also need to protect them. The status of migrants should be a secondary issue after the well-being of each one of our migrant brothers and sisters. We must guarantee their protection, beginning with their place of origin and continuing through their journey and their arrival at their destination. Therefore, I insist that we need to safeguard these migrants through proper consular care, an assurance of their right to attain personal documents, access to equitable justice, and the essential protection of their lives.

All governments should first welcome and then protect migrants. Next, migrants must be helped forward. In opening the doors to them, I ask that we promote a culture of care that is holistic—that they would be given access to resources that will help them flourish in all ways intended by the Creator for his beloved humanity.

I speak of access to work and healthcare, education and rest, religion and housing. Although migrant brothers and sisters suffer from the definite lack of one or more of these rights, depriving them of access to these speaks more of the society that welcomes them than those they are coming from.

I am reminded of the verse in the Acts of the Apostles: "The inhabitants treated us with unusual kindness" (28:2). This refers to how Paul was received in Malta, a land that has been welcoming since then, as I saw this last year. Our challenge is to achieve an "unusual" cordiality and make this the norm. Let us make it a daily practice to open our arms to our brothers and sisters and offer humane treatment.

To accomplish this, it is vital to have systems in place to help migrants when they arrive. Remember that integration does not mean assimilation, leading to suppression and forgetting one's cultural identity. No. The path to integration contributes to a greater knowledge of one another. And for this, we appeal to our leaders to grant access to citizenship to long-term residents and to collaborate with nongovernmental organizations and all people of goodwill toward their integration. In some countries exciting projects are being debated to give the right to citizenship to those students who finish their studies.

At the same time, those who welcome them are called to help them in holistic human care. Those who are welcomed are asked to follow the norms of the nation that they immigrate to, such as respect for the identity of the country.

We still have time to build a future enriched by diversity and intercultural relations. The Acts of the Apostles has a passage that makes me think of integration, harmony, and love: "Parthians, Medes and Elamites; people from Mesopotamia, Judaea and Cappadocia, Pontus and Asia, Phrygia and Pamphylia, Egypt and the parts of Libya round Cyrene; residents of Rome—Jews and proselytes alike—Cretans and Arabs, we hear them preaching in our own language about the marvels of God" (2:9–11). This is how the Scriptures speak of the inhabitants of Jerusalem who heard the preaching of salvation on the day in which the Church was "baptized" on Pentecost, immediately followed by the descent of the Holy Spirit.

It is Politics that has the necessary tools to build a culture of encounter with the migrants, that must stand up against the globalization of indifference that threatens to determine how they are treated.

I would like to highlight the willingness shown in recent times by the people and government of Poland to give space to thousands of people forced to leave Ukraine due to the war, many times even opening up their homes. Lebanon, Malta, and Greece are other nations that have worked with open hearts toward migrants. It is essential, nonetheless, that we do not leave such countries abandoned on the front lines of these conflicts. I am very concerned about the consequences of the war in Ukraine that could lead to a food crisis. We must speak frankly and respectfully to all the nations implicated in these problems—whether it be a nation of origin, transit, or reception—to find new and sustainable solutions with great audacious creativity.

The Scriptures remind us, "Remember always to welcome strangers, for by doing this, some people have entertained angels without knowing it" (Hebrews 13:2). Today, faithfulness to the Gospel means to welcome, protect, help, and integrate. How much pain do we experience when we see nations and even whole regions that were built on the rich cornerstone of migration now turn to build walls! It is concerning to see countries at a higher level of development seek to subcontract the management of their borders and give decisive power to the countries involved in the very conflicts that displace our brothers and sisters. They claim to reject them with unsullied hands despite the fact that every lost life of a brother or sister who crosses the desert, the ocean, or a territory full of dangers should weigh on their minds.

The Scriptures instruct us, "You will not molest or oppress aliens, for you yourselves were once aliens in Egypt" (Exodus 22:20). How can it be that nations with a long Christian tradition, with recurring speeches on the need for human rights, look away and ignore what is happening in the camps where these migrants are forced to live? These situations do not occur in far-off places. They are happening today near our shores. I have heard recorded testimonies speaking of places of torture and the sale of humans. We witness the suffering of our brothers and sisters before us and we cannot remain silent.

Closing ourselves off in our cultures does not contribute to the integration of our brothers and sisters; instead, it staves off the possible enrichment of their experiences. Persons, not numbers! A great author from my homeland pointed out, "Universal history is that of a single human."[3] The stories of our brothers and sisters help us understand ourselves and the world that surrounds us. We will never be able to hear them if we do not take the first step to recognize them.

The other side of the need *"to know* in order *to understand"*[4] is the more palpable and growing danger of xenophobia toward migrants and refugees, which we must be very aware of. Therefore, let us work together and endeavor that these discriminatory and xenophobic reactions in the nations that welcome migrants do not continue to grow, especially in those nations that have a long Christian history.

Often, these rejections suffered by those migrants fleeing toward a better future run the risk of fracturing modern society. These harmful rejections, whether by action or by omission, are encouraged by those in leadership or by social media.

In a global culture with an ever-growing emphasis on individualism and disposability, modern society is even more susceptible to xenophobic and racist speech settling within it. Amid this significant crisis of human values, each person who does not uphold the standards of physical, mental, or social health runs the risk of being marginalized or excluded. Therefore, a change of attitude is necessary: to go from indifference and fear to sincere acceptance of others.

I would like to turn now to social media. It plays an essential role in the responsibility toward migrants. I ask for stereotypes to be unmasked, offering correct information instead of false news, but even more to describe with honesty and moral integrity the nobility of the majority of immigrants. The stories of migrants who have achieved great success in their new homes never equal the amount of space dedicated to those who have committed crimes.

Even in my own homeland of Argentina, there is still great xenophobia against migrants. The native people speak of second-class peoples, those *who come from barbarism,* of *los bolitas, los paraguas,* or *los cabecita negra.** We need to move away from making a nation a mere adjective. This disqualifies them and puts up boundaries. Or we see cases of subtle xenophobia, in which undocumented workers are exploited in the workplace. This occurs in both rural and urban areas.

How can we develop antidotes to this type of hate speech and xenophobia?

Migrants and refugees not only endure terrible suffering before beginning their new lives; in many cases, in the new cities and countries, they must carry the cross of being relegated to second-class citizens and exposed to all types of dangers.

For example, I think of minors who are forced to travel alone, without the care and company of their parents, and who are left at the mercy of their traffickers. We must create awareness campaigns so they do not fall into networks of exploitation through which they become initiated into prostitution, trapped within the cruel pornography industry, enslaved as child workers, recruited to be child soldiers, involved in the drug trade, or ensnared in other forms of delinquency.

Sadly, these terrible situations trap not only children but also adults. Often these adults are condemned to long periods in which they do not have legal status, thus being exposed to abuse and exploitation in the workforce. Many times their desires to integrate are reduced to the possibility of getting jobs that are dangerous, dirty, or denigrating. Many of these vulnerable migrants and workers, along with their families, are excluded from access to the national programs of healthcare, disease preven-

* Argentine pejorative words for Bolivians, Paraguayans, and people of indigenous heritage.

tion, treatment, financial and psychological protection, and social services.

The pandemic, which is just now ending in many places in the world, only increased the challenges facing migrants. During the necessary times of isolation at the beginning of this health crisis, many of the essential workers were migrants, and yet they were not given the benefits of economic aid programs, basic health attention, and vaccines.

It is urgent that we find better solutions for these disparities. Let us not forget that these migrant families are a crucial part of our communities in our globalized world, yet in too many nations, these migrant workers are denied benefits and stability in their family lives due to legal hindrances.

Before the Great Jubilee of 2000, holy John Paul II included displaced peoples among the seemingly endless consequences of wars, conflicts, genocides, and ethnic cleansings that marked the twentieth century. As we draw closer to the 2025 Jubilee, we face the sad reality that in 2020 alone, many millions of people were displaced within their own nation.[5]

In this new century, there has not been a profound change: armed conflicts and other forms of organized violence keep provoking the displacement of people within and outside their nation's borders. In addition, thousands of people tearfully flee wars, persecution, human rights violations, and political and social instability that make life within their country or region impossible. For this reason, in the name of God, I ask that we open the doors to migrants and refugees.

7

In the name of God, I ask that greater participation of women in society be promoted and encouraged

✝

"Women of the entire universe, whether Christian or non-believing, you to whom life is entrusted at this grave moment in history, it is for you to save the peace of the world."[1] Some fifty years ago, the holy Paul VI directed his special message to women across the world in which he set the foundation for the Church to recognize their essential role in society. Since then, advancements have been made in this direction, yet much is left to do. Within our own Church, we are beginning to start processes to recognize women's actual participation.

We have called women to have an active role in the world for years, yet sadly, still today, we must add to this call pleas for their integrity to be respected. Confronted with the plague of violence that so many women face, we must determinedly raise our voices to end femicide.

I call for the end of the horror of human trafficking and of public policies that force women to choose between their profession and motherhood. Professional goals and motherhood should not be opposing life purposes for women.

Having in my heart all the women who have been murdered

just for the fact that they were women, I ask for women's lives, as I do for all human life, to be respected and treated with integrity from conception to natural death.

Across decades of examples, reality has shown us that women hold influential societal positions and can change the system. Over various fields such as economics and Politics, millions of women have taken center stage for the incredible work they have done. Innovative approaches, superior social sensibility, greater empathy, and a perspective for care as a guiding principle have provided clear evidence of the need for greater participation of women in society. This is a sign of hope as we look to the future.

One example is the coronavirus, which seemed to intensify and make more apparent the dozens of problems to which we are accustomed. It showed that "the countries with women as presidents or prime ministers have on the whole reacted better and more quickly than others, making decisions swiftly and communicating them with empathy."[2]

This step forward is good news. For years, women were called to opine and intervene in the public sphere on exclusively "feminine" issues or those considered "light": the most common practice on television was for women to speak of motherhood, fashion, or entertainment. In addition, if there was a feminine presence in political cabinets, she would speak on issues related to children, social assistance, or equal opportunities.

For this reason, it is excellent to see women at the highest levels of business, occupying first place for bestsellers in literature, and becoming true gurus of the world economy. In addition, more nations have had a female leader or presidential candidate in recent years, showing less disparity in the current makeup of governments.

Another example that comes to mind to illustrate that the feminine perspective not only enriches society but also makes better men is that of prisons. Prisons led by women function better than those managed by men. Women have a unique touch and a knack for seeing the whole process, from the trial to reentry into society, which always must be our end goal. I do not know if there are statistics to compare the success of reentry of those who spent their time in jails directed by women and those who spent their time in ones led by men. It would be interesting. I base this idea of female care on what I have seen while visiting prisons: how women seek to relocate detained people to give them better opportunities. Perhaps it is due to maternal instincts or simply an issue of empathy and perspective. It is an observation worth digging deeper into to see if there is actual evidence for this.

One thing I value about women, specifically in the realm of decision-making, is their practical and realistic outlook, which escapes the purview of men. I have seen this so many times as archbishop of Buenos Aires and as pope. I tend to take advice more from women on governmental and administrative issues. I see the female genius at work in that gentleness and tenderness, which provide an added value to their participation. I hope this continues to grow more and more in all facets of society. Our world needs female leadership, skills, intuitions, and dedication.

The recognition of the role of women in society is not a novel concept in the Church, not in the least. Let us think of the Virgin Mary and the fundamental role she played in the history of salvation.

When debating the role of women in the Church, one key concept is not to confuse the role with the position. The discussion on places for women cannot be reduced to mere functionalism, statistics about their growing participation in leadership, or their presence in places of power.

In the first place, the feminine role in the Church luckily exceeds what the Vatican or the structure of the Roman Curia represents. I have tried to create places to appoint women so that they can effectively fulfill their functions. We are growing in this, yet there is a long way to go. It is not simply appointing women to a top office. A whole cultural shift must occur to value and recognize women in their work. We come from a long tradition behind the Vatican walls in which the assignment of women to leading positions was looked at with distrust. Therefore, the opening up of this process to women must also be accompanied by a cultural revolution that can lead to a permanent change.

Another point for debate is the role of women in the Church in helping us rethink what we mean by *Church*. There is a certain level of participation that women have had in Church life for centuries.

In whole sections of the periphery—and I think of the example of the Amazon region—women lead and walk alongside entire Church communities. How many Catholic schools are led by women around the world? The same can be said about Catholic hospitals, including the Vatican pediatric hospital, Bambino Gesù Hospital, whose director is doing excellent work.

Indigenous mothers or mothers in the poorest neighborhoods in Latin America and other similar latitudes who have been charged with sharing and keeping the faith are also part of the Church. I think of a Paraguayan mother who lifted her nation and was able to keep the Gospels aflame following the *Triple Alianza* massacre at the end of the nineteenth century. In Latin America, in a particular way, the Church sees in women a reserve of potential that can be born over and over again.

"In fact, there has never been a time in her history when the faith was not passed on in mother tongues, passed on by mothers and grandmothers. Yet, part of the painful legacy we are now confronting stems from the fact that indigenous grandmothers were prevented from passing on the faith in their own language and culture."[3]

Just as in society on a broader scale, the role of women in the

Church is fundamental and indispensable. Even in the Gospels, we see that the first witnesses of the resurrection of Christ were women. In my first press conference as pope in 2013, I held that the Virgin Mary is more important than the Apostles, Bishops, Deacons, and Priests.[4]

This statement is valid and asks how we can rise to the occasion by opening more substantial space for women in the Church. But, at the same time, we must avoid exposing women to a culture that cannot integrate and respect their style and uniqueness.

The female sensibility is something that we must protect. All forms of violence against women are unacceptable. Beatings, murder, trafficking, abuses, and sexual exploitation in the workplace are grave sins since they go first against the dignity of women and second against all of society. Even more so, they are wounds to the body of Christ. These situations of extreme violence, for which there can be no excuse, coexist alongside other practices, of which we are not fully conscious and to which we cannot permit any more social acceptance: the domestic worker who is not being paid a complete compensation package; the working woman who has to choose between being a mother or keeping her job; the pay gap between men and women; the conditions that generate economic disparity. We all must have an iron will to stop violence against women.

The disposable culture we live in, marked by the globalization of indifference, has multiplied instances of abuse toward women. Mistreatment can manifest itself in many ways and even lead to homicide, yet it has an unending reach into daily life. With sadness, I reiterate the words poured out in *Fratelli Tutti*, where I posited that "the organization of societies worldwide is still far from reflecting clearly that women possess the same dignity and identical rights as men."[5]

We are undergoing a period of greater awareness of women's

rights, which inexplicably is accompanied by indicators that point to an upsurge in violence against women. This is now called femicide, which in many legal systems has come to be typified as a crime with specific characteristics. Yet cases of violence against women are propagating worldwide with no distinction for social class, race, or age.

It is inexcusable that in the twenty-first century, women are still considered second-class citizens in many places. There is a cultural root to this, leading to even more forms of violence. The base of all this is cultural, transcending any border between nations.

According to a recent report, every day more than one hundred girls and women are murdered by a relative or person who is close to them.[6] Many countries in the first world, such as in Europe, contribute to this daily statistic. Femicide has reached the status of a slow-drip pandemic.

Yet without going to the extreme example of murder, which is an outrage, we allow other forms of violence. Often women are assaulted, beaten, raped, or led to prostitution. One example is human trafficking, which reduces women to a piece of merchandise for sale. Not only is it one of the cruelest forms of violence, in which lives are turned into products, but it also attests to how this disposable culture is manifested. In addition, human trafficking points to comprehensive symptoms of men's power over women, even at the highest levels of society.

Trafficking is the supply chain of death. There is a whole route in which various modern problems overlap (poverty, migration, and slavery). In its most public form, prostitution reduces women and girls to mere providers of pleasure.

Let us think about those women who flee from hunger and wars only to fall into the hands of human trafficking. These women escape from poor areas and are ensnared with the promise of a better future or a paying job, only to arrive in the new country to have their passports taken away and be forced into prostitution. Once on the streets or in conditions of slavery, they work under the complicity of the police, who coerce these young women to work. If they do not make money, they are beaten or made to endure other forms of abuse.

Many women have the courage to rebel against this violence that works against them—violence we could call systemic. Men are compelled to combat every violent act committed against women and girls. This applies especially to men who frequent prostitutes, and I here take one of the mottos of women who fight against this specific calvary: "Without clients there is no trafficking."

Women have the same dignity as men. Yet, on every continent and in each nation, the international community must not continue to passively overlook the dramatic consequences of relational systems based on discrimination and submission—systems that subject thousands of women and girls each year to forced marriages, domestic slavery, and other attacks on their dignity. One of these attacks is female genital mutilation. Close to three million young women are at risk of this intervention each year, many times in conditions that are hazardous to their health.[7] This practice, which causes women to suffer humiliation and is a grave attack against their physical well-being, extends across various regions of the world. In the name of God, let us stop this and all forms of violence against women.

To achieve true equality, it is not enough to stop physical violence against women. There is still a long way to go when it comes to the rights of women, especially economic rights.

A "demographic winter" is sneaking into our societies, if it has not already arrived in many places. Among the various reasons, specialists point to concrete blocks in the path of women who want to start a family without abandoning their professional development. While the role of women is critical in the management of home life, the solution is not to "cut their wings" so that they do not have to stop caring for their families; instead, we must have state-organized policies that guarantee maternal leaves or incentives to bring children into the world. Children should not be synonymous with losing one's job or seeing one's career harmed.

We need measures that incentivize birth so that women don't have to "hide their bellies" in the workplace. Children are the hope that makes all people new. For this reason, I am glad that many nations have made laws, defined as "unique and national" subsidies, to subsidize families for every child born. I have heard of other countries with similar measures that calculate the years of child-rearing for the distribution of government pensions.

These ideas are not new positions for the Church. Saint John Paul II promoted these ideas already in 1981 when he said, "In the conviction that the good of the family is an indispensable and essential value of the civil community, the public authorities must do everything possible to ensure that families have all those aids—economic, social, educational, political and cultural assistance—that they need in order to face all their responsibilities in a human way."[8]

I am reminded of the poem of a famous Latin American author who expresses the idea that women pouring out their love and care for their family is the greatest remedy against loneliness and other ailments of this world:

This is the desolate night
from the mountains to the sea.
But I, who rock you,
I am not alone!

The night sky will be desolate
if the moon falls into the sea.

But I, she who holds you,
I am not alone!

It is a desolate world
and flesh goes about sadly.
But I, she who presses you closely,
I am not alone!
—*Gabriela Mistral, "Yo no tengo soledad"*

In the last few years, the pandemic has made clear how economic crises affect women, and it has reminded us of the need for programs to assist women in motherhood. The programs must seek to assist them holistically in their development. I have said that "women urgently need to be helped in caring for their children and not be discriminated against in terms of pay and work, or with the loss of work because they are women."[9] We must be guided by the conviction that if we can provide women with these favorable conditions, they will be able to decisively contribute to the reconstruction of the economy and future societies. Women make the world a more beautiful and a more inclusive place.

Still, amid these problematic situations, women have made a way to move history forward. I am not exaggerating when I say there are thousands of everyday examples of women raising their children alone, which continue to be a fount of inspiration for millions of people worldwide.

Women have a unique sensibility for social situations; there is commitment and generosity, which we rarely see in men. *Babette's Feast* is a Danish film I like very much. Through a series of actions by the main female character, we see a metaphor of fraternity and witness how one person can change reality solely by caring for others. I think it is an example of the female sensitivity to care for others and of women's service to the common good.

This sensibility is often best prepared to lead movements of struggle and revitalization. As a result, we have seen resistance, especially in leading nonviolent activities, such as that shown by Leymah Gbowee and thousands of Liberian women. In recent years, these women, with their prayers and peaceful protests, advocated for peace negotiations when the conflict in Liberia was at its highest levels, leading to the conclusion of the second Liberian civil war.

Servant of God Dorothy Day fought for social justice in the United States in the twentieth century and made the plight of the oppressed her own. Dorothy Day was the founder of the Catholic Worker movement and is often made invisible by wider historiography for the mere fact of being a woman. However, her social activism, passion for justice, and commitment to the cause of the oppressed were directly inspired by the Gospels, her faith, and the examples of the saints.

Geneviève Jeanningros is a French nun who lives here in Rome and whom I admire. She comes every week to my Wednesday audiences, whether it is cold or hot. She does terrific work with the poor and the sick on the outskirts of the city. In 2015 I had the chance to visit Jeanningros and her team, and I was touched by their great effort for the needy. You can perceive in them a religious sensibility.

I have recently been told of another woman from Latin America who, moved by her faith and sensitivity, embarked on a transforming mission for her country. The Honduran María Rosa Leggol, during her seventy years as a Franciscan religious sister, helped more than 87,000 children out of poverty and abuse. Today, many of these children are lawyers, businesspeople, and doctors who now have a career because they had a helping hand during their childhood. This is the intuition to act at the right time and place. Sister María Rosa died during the pandemic. Apparently, she was hardheaded and escaped from the hospital to work with her children as soon as she got cleared from Covid-19.

As I review the efforts of women who have led History forward—History with a capital *H*—I cannot forget the organization *Madres y Abuelas de Plaza de Mayo.** They are a great example of nonviolence, as well as maternal love. I have always told the *Madres y Abuelas* that they can count on me. Because of all they have undergone, the most profound type of suffering, these women have my inexhaustible help. It is the pain of a mother. They suffered something so inhumane: the disappearance of their children without ever seeing their bodies or where they were buried. The military dictatorship in Argentina from 1976–1983 tore their children away from them. It is an extreme experience for a mother. Despite this pain, they organized and advanced many of their pleas, always in a pacificist fashion. We must accompany them, respect their pain, hold their hands, and walk alongside them.

We must all participate in opening new spaces for women if we want to see a fertile and creative future. The Social Doctrine of the Church recognizes that "the persistence of many forms of discrimination offensive to the dignity and vocation of women in the area of work is due to a long series of conditioning that penalizes women, who have seen 'their prerogatives misrepresented' and themselves 'relegated to the margins of society and even reduced to servitude.'"[10]

For this reason, I ask in the name of God that we promote greater female participation in society. Amid a diverse host of humiliating circumstances that we have not overcome worldwide, I ask to stop the murder and injury of women's dignity. For these actions are acts of harm to Christ himself.

* Mothers and Grandmothers of Plaza de Mayo.

8

In the name of God, I ask that the growth of poor countries be allowed and encouraged

✟

The ten wealthiest people on our planet doubled their fortunes during the pandemic. The richest 1 percent of the world holds 32 percent of all wealth.[1]

Although at the beginning of the twentieth century there was a similar concentration of income as now, when we include all of the world's poorest people, they do not account for even 8 percent of the current global wealth.[2]

The rich are getting richer, and the poor are getting poorer. This current system kills and excludes people and concentrates wealth. In this context, it is vital to shift from an economy that puts the idol of money at its center to one that centers on people, thinking of their relationships and dignity. For this reason, in the name of God, I ask that the growth of poor countries be allowed and encouraged.

The diagnosis made by analysts emboldens us to question all ideological attempts to justify these inequalities. We must say no "to an economy of exclusion and inequality."[3] The end of the pandemic is an opportunity for us to leave behind this way of thinking about the economy, the world, and the logic of power and instead think of ourselves as members of the same family.

The numbers from the last two years show the failure of a

trickle-down theory that suggests that the majority of people have to watch as the cup of those who have the most fills up, while hoping for tiny drops to fall on the least fortunate. The cups of the powerful are too full, and the rest are more and more thirsty for dignity and justice. Meanwhile, a "culture of prosperity deadens us"[4] and generates a society of passive spectators who stand by and watch the increasing growth of inequality. The good news is that we can say enough is enough.

This is a sick system because while the world is getting richer year after year, the poor are getting increasingly more impoverished due to our unending harm toward our Common Home. Hundreds of millions of people live each day in conditions of extreme poverty: no food, no home, no healthcare, and no electricity. A list of "nos" in a world of cynicism. This is the only way we can describe this world in which, according to studies of international organizations, almost six million children die each year in extreme poverty.[5] The deaths of our brothers and sisters due to poverty are avoidable. Similarly, we are not condemned to the unjust distribution of wealth, to which we all contribute.

Now that the pandemic is waning in many nations, there is talk of the "new normal." We should not tolerate these scandalous statistics as normal. The recovery of the world economy should not come at the cost of the poor majority, as it has in the past through a system in which a minority of people gain incredible wealth. This economic and social model we are following is inequitable and unsustainable.

The redesign of the economic and social systems of the future is not something we should leave to market forces. The Congregation for the Doctrine of the Faith and the Dicastery for Promoting Integral Human Development laid this down in a document, stating, "Economic and financial issues draw our attention today as never before because of the growing influence of financial markets on the material well-being of most of humankind. What is needed, on the one hand, is an appropriate regulation of the dynamics of the markets and, on the other hand, a clear ethical foundation that assures a well-being realized through the quality of human relationships rather than merely through economic mechanisms that by themselves cannot attain it."[6]

We should not have a problem ending poverty in this world of rich possibilities. But what has happened to humanity when we do not begin each day thinking of new ways to include, feed, heal, and clothe the lowest in society rather than excluding them? In this world, it is up to us to pick which type of system we want to prioritize: one that deals with and eliminates injustice or one that justifies and expands it.

This system of death is part of what I have called the globalization of indifference and the disposable culture. In his encyclical *Sollicitudo Rei Socialis*, the holy John Paul II spoke of "evil mechanisms" that condition our world. The reasons are not merely economic or political but also moral. For my predecessor, it had to do with "structures of sin."[7]

When we speak of the need for a new international financial architecture, it is precisely this: we need new structures. Unfortunately, the structure under which this system was built may not be the most suitable way to get us out of this current situation. A new structure must be more generous with Mother Earth, pay attention to the development of local communities, and be more concerned with subsidiarity and investment in education and infrastructure, especially in places overlooked by the international community in the past years.

We have the responsibility of ending economic injustices. Undoubtedly, there are different levels of responsibility, but injustice makes claims on all of us. So, we need an iron commitment by governments and multilateral credit agencies, from the private to the public sector, to all the players in this social network.

There are situations in the current international financial structure that are considered legal, yet in some cases, we must call them immoral. These include the usurious rates for developing nations, judicial corruption, and the speculation of vulture funds, the overattentive care of powerful multinational corporations in their interests in specific countries, and the systems of tax evasion and havens that affect wholesale public accounts. In this context, financial groups and international lending agencies must ensure that the poorest nations are not left broke, having to pay back predatory loans before attending to the needs of their people.

There is a shared responsibility to assist impoverished nations in their development and to forgive debt for the most indebted countries. In the same way, there should be a shared responsibility in assisting with loans at a national level, many of which are likely not legitimate and are incurred by governments who are incapable of paying them off. In these cases, the national leaders take on these debts and end up mortgaging the future of their nations for years to come.

Far from finding solutions, it seems this problem is becoming more prominent as the interest from these debts consumes the resources of these nations—resources that could be put toward social programs or vital infrastructure, allowing the nations to take a step forward. In 1991, holy John Paul II emphasized the gravity of this situation by stating, "It cannot be expected that the debts which have been contracted should be paid at the price of unbearable sacrifices. In such cases it is necessary to find—as in fact is partly happening—ways to lighten, defer or even cancel the debt, compatible with the fundamental right of peoples to subsistence and progress."[8]

This does not mean that we should not respect the principle of paying debts that have been legitimately acquired, but we should refuse to accept the unbalanced method in which coun-

tries are required to fulfill their payments, which is the same in
the poorest nations as in the wealthiest countries. We need a
method that would not compromise the subsistence and growth
of the poorest nations. For this reason, a new international financial structure must also focus on the morality of debts.

We need a humane perspective centered on holistic human
development. We cannot look at the money spent by these developing nations to fulfill their debts solely as a percentage of their
gross domestic product. When these resources are spent to pay
off debt, schools are not built and hospitals are without supplies.
The social fabric becomes frayed and unravels for generations to
come. Forcing the payment of debts with funds that should be
destined to rebuild a nation is morally deplorable, especially
when the rights to the loans are bought by hedge funds or
private-equity funds that make these decisions based on financial
speculation.

Another troubling situation is that of offshore companies.
Each year billions of dollars that should be allocated to paying
taxes that finance healthcare and education are accumulated in
these tax havens, which stains the nation's dignity and hinders
support from its citizens. Even worse, often these havens are
merely for the laundering of ill-gotten money, which takes resources from the economy.

The Congregation for the Doctrine of the Faith and the Dicastery for Promoting Integral Human Development observed
that "the accumulated private wealth of some elites in the fiscal
havens is almost equal to the public debt of the respective countries. This highlights how, in fact, at the origin of that debt there
are often economic losses created by private persons and un-
loaded on the shoulders of the public system. Moreover, it is
noted that important economic players tend to follow, often with
the collusion of the politicians, a practice of division of the
losses."[9]

The growth of poor countries must be allowed and encouraged. The current interrelatedness of the world makes it possible for reasonable policies and agreed-upon reduction of public debt to be not only a solution for the countries directly affected but also a medicine for the entire international economic system. This would avoid the "contagion" of potentially systemic crises, a condition that further delays the consensus needed for putting the economy at the service of the common good of people.

At the same time, I am happy to see Popular Movements asking for a profound change, not only on an economic level but also with a renewed systemic focus to promote actual holistic human development. I refer to these Popular Movements as a multifaceted group of those who have the scent of the barrio, the people, and struggle. These Popular Movements are groups of like-minded people, associations, workers often in precarious or informal situations, and victims of the daily disposable society. They are examples of the seeds for a different future, an essential piece in true social transformation. They have emerged to show a way forward so that things can change.

They do this by reminding us of the deep roots that speak of the common good and the universal destination of goods based on the Social Doctrine of the Church. God wanted these goods of life to be for all people. For this reason, Land, Home, Work, and Food must be within reach of all people. To say it plainly, Land, Home, Work, and Food should be fundamental rights and indispensable prerequisites for democracy, not merely an idealistic goal.

I think it is pertinent to touch briefly on these four claims made by these movements.

Land

The first root of the universal destination of goods is that of land. "God gave the earth to the whole human race for the sustenance of all its members, without excluding or favouring anyone. . . . *The Church's social teaching moreover calls for recognition of the social function of any form of private ownership* that clearly refers to its necessary relation to the common good. . . ."[10]

Today, the Popular Movements' voices call for the promotion of new methods of communal ownership of the land, following ancestral lines of some indigenous communities and working for the sustainable and harmonious use of the resources of Mother Earth. One such method in many nations is the association model of small producers, who become the primary food source. These producers have the experience of growing crops and caring for the land in a way that keeps it fertile by utilizing biodiversity, which is different from the models that use monoculture in great tracts of land.

Just as we debate new ways for small producers to access the land, organized in models of family agriculture or small communities, we must ensure they are taken care of so they are not driven out by the massive territories of great landowners. This model is often accompanied by the desire for land reform to solve some of these problems. My predecessors held the position of land reform, making sure that the right to the land is guaranteed to all people: "Land Reform is assigned a vital role in the eradication of hunger and poverty from the country sides of the world."[11] Already at the Second Vatican Council, with the constitution *Gaudium et Spes,* the Conciliar Fathers remarked that "in many underdeveloped regions there are large or even extensive rural estates which are only slightly cultivated or lie completely idle for the sake of profit, while the majority of the people either are without land or have only very small fields, and, on the other hand, it is evidently urgent to increase the productivity of the fields."[12]

Home

In my encyclical letter *Fratelli Tutti,* I recalled the words of Saint John Chrysostom, who said, "Not to share our wealth with the poor is to rob them and take away their livelihood. The riches we possess are not our own, but theirs as well."[13] This observation is in line with the idea outlined by Saint Gregory the Great, who said, "When we provide the needy with their basic needs, we are giving them what belongs to them, not to us."[14]

Today, we live in a paradox that is shaped by a disordered system, and we are now being awakened to it by Popular Movements. More and more people now live in large, overcrowded cities, while there are empty homes in many of the cities of our nations. The Italian Cuban author Italo Calvino described this with great certainty: "The crisis of the overgrown city is the other side of the crisis of the natural world."[15]

I have followed with significant interest proposals to use these empty homes, as well as the great tracts of land that are not in use. However, since the *"Christian tradition has never recognized the right to private property as absolute and untouchable,"*[16] if it has to do with the political function of the property, local governments have to initiate it.

A lack of a holistic policy exists for those in need who have the right to a decent home. This often results from actions of a housing market that extends across many nations. We see luxury homes with completely automized amenities barely removed from large tracts of precarious housing without access to basic sanitation, water, and electricity. This problem and others generate a severe concern for the growing impossibility of young people owning their own homes.

Work

The next topic is work, and I want to expand on my ideas about the "biggest issue" of our day.[17] All intiatives that seek to make the system more humane and put the human being at the center must be based on creating a diversified source of jobs. It is one of today's most significant challenges, with the intertwined responsibilities of governments, businesses, unions, and Popular Movements.

The many crises of the twenty-first century have resulted in grave consequences for many developed nations, including some in Europe, where most youths do not have jobs. In the rest of the world, unemployment assistance programs have grown to respond to the overwhelming impossibility of absorbing millions of people who have been excluded from the job market.

Work is one of the main tools for bestowing dignity on human beings. Of course, there are extraordinary circumstances—such as the pandemic—in which nations might need special help, especially among the most vulnerable populations. However, governmental assistance programs must be seen as temporary and not definitive solutions. Welfare policies must be precisely that: a policy, not a way of life. Subsidies clearly offer help in accessing food and other goods, but it is work that guarantees dignity.

How do we develop policies that are centered on making sure that all individuals have the chance to contribute their abilities and effort? To complicate matters, we are having these debates while robotization and the use of artificial intelligence threaten the stability of the labor market for millions worldwide.

At the same time, there is a long list of tasks that people do without a salary, whether it is caring for an elderly family member, caring for children, or even participating in volunteer work. Often this is the case for women. For this reason, I have expressed my favor for a universal basic income that could make these situations more equitable. A tool such as this could discourage industries that are aware of the extensive unemployment index in some countries from paying extremely low salaries. These low-paying industries see the workers as disposable, saying, "If you do not accept this salary, there are thousands that can replace you."

Along the same line, I have talked about reducing the workday or workweek. Pilot programs have been launched in many countries to try a four-day workweek. Perhaps this initiative can help distribute the available work hours, generating solidarity among employees and reducing the armies of unemployed people who are worth more than the small salaries offered.

Food

Beyond the unequal access to Land, Home, and Work, we cannot shift our gaze away from the grave inequities in the global distribution of food. We live in a rich world where people should not need to be condemned to poverty, including a lack of housing, decent salary, and prosperous land to live on. We should also not resign ourselves to the fact that many of our brothers and sisters are dying because they do not have access to the necessary food to keep them alive.

The world produces enough food for eleven billion people, and the current world population is close to eight billion people. Yet according to a 2022 report titled "The State of Food Security and Nutrition in the World," prepared by five agencies of the United Nations (FAO, WFP, IFAD, WHO, and UNICEF), the number of people who suffer from hunger in the world reached between 702 and 828 million in 2021. This number is an increase of about 46 million people since 2020 and 150 million since before the outbreak of the coronavirus pandemic.[18] This is a scandalous situation that shows that the world is losing sight of the objective of ending hunger, food insecurity, and malnutrition in all forms by 2030.

It is utterly cruel that despite the fact that there is enough food, people do not have access to it and there are regions of the world where food is wasted, either by being thrown out, consumed in excess, or dedicated to something other than feeding human beings.

We cannot permit any more market-centered plans when thinking about bread for our brothers and sisters.

What tools can we use to guarantee safe and continuous access to food for all humanity? How can we work toward global food security, even during the war in Ukraine, when the first few weeks of the conflict caused a spike in many commodities?

It is calculated that about one-third of all food produced is wasted. Often this is due to poor distribution or the discarding of food that is grown because its appearance does not meet a certain criteria. However, we cannot go on like this. When food is wasted, it is as if it were being robbed from the tables of the poor.

Hunger continues to be one of the greatest plagues impacting our world, with millions of children dying every year. According to UNICEF, millions of children face malnutrition each day, which has lasting effects on their cognitive development. Lack of food causes diabetes and cardiovascular diseases, among other problems.[19] We must act now. We are finally overcoming the pandemic, yet we are facing other hurdles. A poem by the American writer Emily Dickinson says:

"Hope" is the thing with feathers
That perches in the soul
And sings the tune without the words
And never stops—at all
—Emily Dickinson, " 'Hope' Is the Thing with Feathers"

Our hope must be placed in a cause that can bring all humanity together: the fight against the silent and lethal evil of hunger. We must mobilize against this without pause.

How we have been relating to money cannot continue. Money must serve and not rule. It must be a means and not an end. We must stop this culture of accumulation and waste to create systems of global solidarity that allow all inhabitants of the planet access to Land, Home, Work, and Food. For this reason, in the name of God, I pray for those poor nations, the discarded and excluded on our planet.

9

In the name of God, I ask for universal access to health services

✝

The pandemic has exposed a global crisis and invites us to ask ourselves how we can get out of it. The spread of Covid-19 on a global level unmasked an unjust system. It has generated all sorts of disparities, with intolerable effects on the well-being of most of the world's population.

The pandemic made our preexisting vulnerabilities more visible and contributed to accelerating and worsening social and environmental situations that have harmed the fabric of humanity. We will not emerge from the crisis the same. For this reason, in the name of God, I ask that we consider this opportunity to universalize access to health services. We need processes that concretely ensure a holistic view of human flourishing that centers the global health situation. In particular, I ask that we pay attention to the weak, the children, and the elderly and that we respect life's dignity in all its phases.

Thanks to technology and the collaboration among various people, we were able to quickly facilitate vaccines to end this pandemic, at least in the nations that had easy and rapid access to them. One aspect we cannot take our eyes off is the injustices that, in many cases, have deepened worldwide. Once more, we see how the poorest and weakest are always the ones who carry the weight of the "deeply interrelated crises like those of the climate, food, the economy and migration."[1]

The distribution of the vaccines and the advance of the inoculation campaigns in different countries showed us the patterns of inequity in the area of health that existed even before the onset of the pandemic.

Vaccines in developed countries, many of them created in laboratories, reached the majority of the adult population quickly. In this way, the countries were able to minimize the cost of their socioeconomic paralysis and begin processes of economic reactivation, resulting in higher indexes of growth.

It was quite the opposite for less-developed nations, who saw reflected in the global distribution of vaccines the same structures impeding their development. Except for a few cases, the vaccine was seen as one more piece of merchandise for international circulation—a problematic attitude that is far from any vision of empathy, solidarity, and fraternity that this global health crisis requires.

At the very beginning of this pandemic, I said in Saint Peter's Square that "no one reaches salvation by themselves."[2] Now, three years since this prayer, the advent of new coronavirus strains should remind us that the whole human family is in the same boat, launching into the tempestuous sea of the pandemic. Only by addressing this current crisis with solutions that give a preferential option for the weak on a global scale can we hope to arrive at a port safely.

I want to highlight the work of various governments that were able to reach high levels of immunization among their people. They did this despite the proliferation of fake news concerning the effectiveness of the vaccines and denial movements that seemed to show coordination on a multinational level. At the same time, there is a long way to go to ensure that the origin of the vaccine is not a motive for dispute or prejudice. We must be earnest in our rejection of the idea that geopolitical goals are more important than science and health.

The vaccines for the coronavirus should be seen as a common good for humanity that marks a path forward to universalizing access to health services. The pandemic left ample evidence of the interrelatedness of the whole human family; therefore, only universal access to treatments for this disease and others should be considered as a global solution.

In this situation, I am grateful for the various efforts in recent times to find new ways of solidarity at a global level. For example, new systems have been put into place to ensure an equal distribution of vaccines, not based on purely economic means but taking into account the needs of all, especially those who are vulnerable and at risk. This type of action serves as the model for similar initiatives with other medicines, especially for people with rare diseases or in need of specialized pediatric procedures, which are often unattainable for some patients.

On many occasions, I defined getting the vaccine as an "act of love" for our neighbor, a fraternal embrace for our brothers and sisters on the path toward ending the pandemic.[3]

The objections to getting vaccinated, many of them totally justifiable for medical conditions of different sorts, run the risk of becoming a type of egoism and lack of empathy toward many people. Many countries still have not recovered from this hit, whether the reasons for the lockdown they adopted were economic or social.

As with other situations of crisis, the majority of people who found themselves without income or with extra difficulties in finding a decent job—or, at the least, state programs to assist them—were the weak, the unprotected, the unemployed, the exploited workers, and the informal sector. Moreover, many of those affected were women. Once again, the pandemic made clear the intolerable inequality of opportunity for women compared to men. In some cases, these situations of need deriving from the pandemic made women easy prey to trafficking and exploitation.

The pandemic elevated the risk of us becoming like Narcissus, the character from ancient mythology who loves only himself and ignores the well-being of others. There is now a spiritual virus that is very contagious, one that turns us into self-focused men and women who see only ourselves and no one else. The reality is that we are responsible for caring for ourselves and our health, which translates to caring for the health of those nearest to us; there is an unequivocal moral obligation. Let us not fall prey to the sirens' songs of a culture of well-being that calls us to care only for ourselves and makes us insensitive to the cries of others. This is the first sure sign of the globalization of indifference.

I want to use the image of the vaccines as a compass that guides us toward our north star, which is the hope of ending this pandemic. As a human family, we are all aboard the same boat; we seek to leave these troubled waters that we have been navigating for the last three years. I am reminded of Abraham, who, in a moment of doubt, turned to God to ask for help in waiting instead of asking for the promised son that had not yet arrived (see Genesis 15:2–6). This passage shows us something beautiful: the prayer to have hope because hope never fails. It is our turn to transform this hope into a sincere and concrete commitment.

For this reason, alongside my plea in the name of God for universalizing access to health services, I ask that we maintain relationships of fraternity and solidarity with our neighbor. Over the last three years, the virus has shown us that the best way of taking care of ourselves is to learn to care for and protect those we have next to us "with a conscious awareness of the neighborhood, the town, the region, and our Common Home."[4]

It is time for us to recognize those scientists who, for months, studied the correct combination to obtain the most effective vaccine. I am thinking of those who were with us during the most critical phase of the pandemic: doctors, nurses, volunteers, and many others who were in the background, away from the limelight and the covers of newspapers. Thank you for your daily commitment and for giving without reservation.

Now that the majority of countries have left behind the worst part of the pandemic and most of the restrictions have been lifted, is it not time for us to think about the idea of medical patents calmly and with an eye toward the future?

Given the possibility of a new global health crisis, which many scientists and experts believe is a plausible scenario in the medium-term, should we not debate with resolve the necessity of having immediate, universal, and homogenous access to medicines? Access to drugs that is not bound by the logic of the market or the interests of big pharmaceutical companies but by policies that save the lives of those who dwell on planet Earth?

Have we not learned our lesson from the undignified inequalities in access to coronavirus vaccines that condemned the most underprivileged of the world to late access? Beyond the number of lives that could have been saved, it is not an insignificant fact that rapid access to vaccines allowed countries to begin to recover economically sooner and, consequently, to provide help for those most affected by the pandemic. In contrast, there is consensus among experts that the economies of less-developed nations will unfortunately take years to recover.

Over five years ago, I said, "If there is one sector in which the culture of waste is most clear in its consequences, it is precisely the health sector."[5] Today, the numbers show that this has only worsened, and for this reason, I must renew my claim that "the business model of the health sector, if it is adopted indiscriminately, instead of optimizing available resources, runs the risk of wasting human lives."[6] I want to recognize one of the most out-standing doctors from my country, who in 2023 would have cel-ebrated his one hundredth birthday. At the end of the twentieth century, he said, "It is essential to organize international coop-eration between the developed and developing nations to fight together for a better society, with greater equality and social jus-tice. This will make possible the respect and defense of the in-alienable rights of human beings to enjoy good health, alongside other social victories."[7]

The pandemic has offered us an opportunity to see health, once and for all, as the right of humanity, rather than with the blinders that reduce humans to mere objects peddled on the market. In *The Man Who Was Thursday*, a novel that perfectly serves as a metaphor for man's pilgrimage on Earth toward his encounter with God, G. K. Chesterton warns us of a possible reality: "The most poetical thing, more poetical than the flowers, more poetical than the stars—the most poetical thing in the world is not being sick."[8] The coronavirus pandemic showed the world that "the most poetical thing in the world is not being sick," and it demonstrated how to help bring this about through equal access to basic cures and medications.

We must not forget, in any case, that the right to health pro-tection is intimately tied to other complex economic, social, and cultural factors. Here I need to return to something I said in my apostolic exhortation *Evangelii Gaudium:* "The need to resolve the structural causes of poverty cannot be delayed, not only for the pragmatic reason of its urgency for the good order of society, but because society needs to be cured of a sickness which is weaken-ing and frustrating it, and which can only lead to new crises."[9]

With the same emphasis with which I have asked for equitable access to health at a global level, I also ask for a reevaluation of how our health systems treat the most vulnerable in our societ-ies. In recent years there has been an accelerated trend, in certain countries, to accept as normal the practice of looking at people with genetic, serious, rare, and terminal illnesses as disposable.

For this reason, in the name of God, I ask for the protection and care of life in all its phases. There is a human life at conception, a life at gestation, a life at birth, a child life, a youth life, an adult life, an elderly and feeble dying life, and eternal life. It is always human life. Also, it is a fragile, sick, hurt, abused, dejected, marginalized, and discarded life. We are called to renew our Christian commitment to protect this life.

As I have said on many occasions, death cannot be seen as a right a patient can appeal to, using common sense with doctors and hospitals that seek to promote a doctrine called "just death." The presence of projects in different stages that promote euthanasia in many nations goes hand in hand with an outlook that does not accept that human life is the greatest gift given to us by God.

Our north star must be continuing to accompany patients with discernment that anchors us in the ethical criteria for the defense of life. Is it not necessary—on the other side of the disposable culture—to talk about issues of palliative care? This focus will never lose its importance because it lifts up the value of life.

I repeat what I said in early 2023 when I highlighted all the help from the medical field in the area of palliative care, which tries to offer all people the best care to live the last stretch of their lives in the most dignified manner possible.

On the other hand, I want to warn us to be aware and not confuse this help with the unacceptable choices that lead to death. We need to accompany those dying but not help them die or assist them in suicide. Life must be respected, cared for, and protected from the moment of conception until the end of life. We need to provide care for the weakest in society, especially the elderly and sick, so they are never merely discarded.

It is important to make clear the difference between embracing death and administering death. It is an ethical principle that involves all of us. A social problem that threatens to grow in many nations is the proposal to plan and accelerate the death of the elderly. Or, in a similar way, to administer the least amount of medication because the patients do not have the means to pay for it. "This is not helping them, it is driving them towards death earlier. This is neither human nor Christian."[10]

The proposal for palliative care must be an answer to those movements that spread euthanasia. In fact, it is based on the teachings of Jesus in the Parable of the Good Samaritan, in which we are told that care is an act of compassion. Care is not to be synonymous with pity or disgust; rather, it is more than this. It is the predisposition to enter into the problem and put ourselves in the place of the other, with the desire to take away the pain of loneliness and anxiety.

Many times the movements for euthanasia are accompanied by projects that seek to legalize abortion and that point to the idea of supposed individual liberties. This can only lead to the exclusion of the most vulnerable members of our human family: children yet to be born, the sick, the elderly, and people with terminal illnesses. A health system will be for all when these people are considered protagonists in the system itself. Therefore, we can evaluate a health system based on its reach in providing care to those with nothing to give back, such as children about to be born and older people approaching death.

These debates are influenced by the different advances in technology that impact bioethics and force us to think calmly and comprehensively about how humanity will walk through these new scenarios. Therefore, I repeat once more my plea that the applications of new biotechnologies are always used to respect human dignity.

I have asked for a global vision of bioethics rooted in social ethics and humanism. Any approach to these topics must have a bioethical outlook that remembers that science, biotechnology, and the medical field were developed to uphold the dignity of people. All this was done through critical effort, and now, in this accelerated rhythm of life, it runs the risk of losing any reference point that is not geared toward utility and profit.

We need Christian answers for the challenges, which are increasingly complicated bioethical questions. We need to recognize these questions and provide solutions to them. We must avoid positions that seek to sweep them under the rug or blindly cheer them on.

These situations are more and more challenging, especially in a context marked by relativism and a disposable culture. These situations demand humility, realism, and a culture of encounter. We must not be afraid to have conversations with people of different positions. Instead, the best path forward is to rely on constructive dialogues that contribute to a mature civic consciousness.

Here I would like to clarify that we do not want to stop technological progress. No; instead, we must walk with it. It is about "protecting human dignity and progress" since "both go together and harmoniously together," as I stated in my prayers of March 2022.[11]

I am reminded of the words of philosopher Romano Guardini that "contemporary man has not been trained to use power well." In my encyclical letter *Laudato Si'*, I brought forward the proposal that this is because "immense technological development has not been accompanied by a development in human responsibility, values and conscience."[12]

For this reason, it is essential to point out that "each age tends to have only a meagre awareness of its own limitations. It is possible that we do not grasp the gravity of the challenges now before us. 'The risk is growing day by day that man will not use his power as he should'; in effect, 'power is never considered in terms of the responsibility of choice which is inherent in freedom' since its 'only norms are taken from alleged necessity, from either utility or security.'"[13]

All these considerations I am developing about health and life would be incomplete if I did not take extra time to speak about the elderly. For in them, we have seen the risk of being discarded, which is only growing in frequency. Paradoxically, there have never before been so many elderly, since life expectancy has increased in many countries.

The deepest Christian roots illustrate to us that the elderly must be taken care of as the treasure of humanity, since in them we find wisdom, always teaching, showing, and offering new things.

It is vital to encourage greater participation of the elderly in social life. I have stated the paradox that those who are fortunate to enter old age have "care plans, but not projects of existence."[14] Universalizing access to health services must include an outlook that rejects the notion that the elderly are disposable.

Not only is the importance of the elderly intrinsic, but they are also the living memory of our society. The elderly have a role to play in transmitting wisdom to our young people. In the back-and-forth dialogue, there are hidden riches that we can aspire to as a mature society that learns from respecting different times. It is a type of conversation that sees the rhythms of life as the best antidote to the frenetic pace of the immediate. This dialogue allows the elderly to share their dreams and the young people to receive them and carry them forward.

Let us not forget that in our social culture, such as in a family, the elderly are the tree's roots: they have all the history there, and the young people are the flowers and fruits of that tree. A poet from my homeland, Francisco Luis Bernárdez, wrote, "That what on the tree flowers / lives from what is buried."[15] If we do not keep alive this sap that comes from the roots, we will never be able to bloom.

And for all these reasons I ask for more equitable access to health services. I do this in the name of God.

10

In the name of God, I ask that
the name of God not be used to incite wars

+

Over fifty years ago, the Conciliar Fathers who had attended Vatican II gifted us with the declaration *Nostra Aetate*. Within it were a series of definitions of the relationship of the Church with other non-Christian religions, including that "universal fraternity excludes all discrimination."[1]

This precept is more relevant today than ever, within and outside Christianity. The challenges of living in a world in which indifference is globalized, living amid a disposable culture, and experiencing a third world war call all of humanity to renew its links of solidarity and fraternity. This charge must mobilize believers of all religions to unite in prayer and action to shape absolute peace. We must be iron-willed in our commitments to work for the universal common good, holistic human development, and the promotion of a culture of encounter. Believers and nonbelievers, Christians and non-Christians, Catholics and non-Catholics are all part of the same human family. Promoting fraternity is not new: the Scriptures tell us that God told Noah to go into the ark with his family before the imminent risk of wholesale human destruction (see Genesis 7:1–4). Today, the risk is not reduced. We face war, pandemics, and economic and environmental crises. Amid these stormy waters, we are all called to get into the boat of fraternity. This way, we can face the challenges before us. I can say without exaggerating that fraternity is the only vehicle we have that will guarantee us a future.

For this reason, I renew my invitation to all religions to walk together to build a world based on solidarity, respectful dialogue, and a daily life founded on a culture of encounter rooted in knowledge. We must unite unanimously and condemn any attempt to use the name of the Almighty to justify any violence and aggression. Let us be doers of peace, revolutionaries of kindness, and bearers of love and mercy.

I reiterate what I warned on one of the trips I made to a place where the majority of citizens were Muslim. There, I held that "the enemy of fraternity is an individualism which translates into the desire to affirm oneself and one's own group above others."[2]

This reminds us that "true religious piety consists in loving God with all one's heart and one's neighbour as oneself. Religious behaviour, therefore, needs continually to be purified from the recurrent temptation to judge others as enemies and adversaries. Each belief system is called to overcome the divide between friends and enemies, in order to take up the perspective of heaven, which embraces persons without privilege or discrimination."[3]

True fraternity is based on a culture of encounter. It is to go "out to sea" with respect, making our differences a way to mutual enrichment and having no excuse to distance ourselves.

Rowing toward this sea of encounters and dialogue with others does not mean we end up assimilating their culture or vice versa. On the contrary, true authentic fraternity assumes the shape of a polyhedron, where each face interacts with the others without losing its identity. It is a form in which, together, all make up a new and enriched figure. Let us think about our cultures and societies with this model in mind.

The path of fraternity is not a shortcut or an easy way forward. But it can be our compass as we navigate together, as humanity, these open seas: it will save us from the storms and tempests.

In moments of hardship, we must make an effort to get close to our brothers and sisters who profess other beliefs or no beliefs. We are in this Common Home and are all called to walk together toward a common future.

Many of us who are older have lived out the consequences of moments in which *fraternity* was a problematic word in the vocabulary of humanity. For this reason, young people must step toward a future of fraternity and solidarity. We want together to help young people write a future that sees people with different beliefs as protagonists. We can share life stories of living in difficult moments and even situations that put us at the edge of hope, but we can also tell of many other instances that preserved fraternity.

We bear the responsibility of leaving young people with a fragmented and polarized world. With this weighty heritage, fraternity seems less like an option and more like an imperative. For this reason, I reiterate, "Either we are brothers and sisters, or everything falls apart."[4]

We are called to be artisans of peace for society. We have within us what is needed to overcome the fears of building a tomorrow that is more fraternal. So let us take the first steps and go out to encounter the other—those who are different from us. Let us put our hands, minds, and hearts into working together. Let us be the change we want to see in the world.

With this objective in mind, during the years I have been the bishop of Rome, I have applied my experience from my time in Buenos Aires. I am referring to interreligious dialogue, which in my home country happens almost naturally and which we have improved over generations. It is not something we learned in the university but in our daily lives. I went to a public school in my early years, and it was indeed a *macedonia* (fruit salad), like those of Italian heritage say. There were children and grandchildren of Spaniards, children of Jewish families, and children from Muslim families and the Middle East. We would share birthdays and religious holidays and play games together at school as one family. This is not something that can be taught, but from the time I was six or seven years old, I grew up with the certainty that the other kids were my equals, friends, and brothers. This is a lesson I have taken with me for the rest of my life.

Ecumenism can be a little more complicated. Within our Catholic homes, we had a closeness with Jews and Muslims, but we did not have that experience with Evangelicals or Presbyterians. Yet this mentality started to grow, maturing into a dialogue. This orientation toward ecumenism was strong at the beginning of the twentieth century, when many important ceremonies had an interreligious and ecumenical character. In other countries, it has been easier to develop this, with ecumenical friendships forged out of conditions of poverty or unity against totalitarian regimes, bringing fraternity to the surface in the face of adversity.

When leaving Rome and going on official visits, I try to promote dialogue with all my brothers and sisters, whether Jewish, Muslim, or of another Christian tradition. In many countries I visit, when I meet with the Catholic faithful of a local church, I think it is crucial to also meet with leaders of other Christian communities and faith traditions.

The reality is that most of the Earth's population define themselves as believers in some form of higher power.[5] There is something on the level of the transcendent that unites us as brothers and sisters. For all peoples of the world, our common shared experience of being believers should be a beginning point for us to seek to have more fruitful encounters. Being practitioners and believers of our different religions is a commonality we all share, and it should beckon us forward into true encounter with one another.

When engaging in interreligious conversation, "Three basic areas, if properly linked to one another, can assist in this dialogue: the duty to respect one's own identity and that of others, the courage to accept differences, and sincerity of intentions."[6] In practice, not sacrificing who we are to please others must be a guiding principle. We must see others as fellow journeyers, and we must always be honest and transparent with one another. Sincere dialogue makes us recognize the rights and liberties of others. This is what we need to have a true fraternal coexistence.

With its fratricidal tendencies, the world today asks us for fraternal conviction—a recommitment to the message of the declaration *Nostra Aetate,* which is very relevant, especially with its ideas of the unity of the human family and the conception of a Church that is open to dialogue with all people: with our fellow Christian brothers and sisters, but also with our siblings who are Muslim and Jewish and with those faithful of all religions.

On the ecumenical front, in our current climate, it is necessary to mark this certainty: we can no longer each walk our own way. The world is demanding unity. In some places, they do not separate Catholics and Protestants when they persecute us, curtail our freedoms, or kill us. On the contrary, the ecumenism of blood makes us siblings before this senselessness. The martyrdom of Christians around the world calls us to accelerate our dialogues and encounters. How many Christian martyrs do we weep for today? Not only is our Church the most attacked today, but the persecution of our brothers and sisters is also greater now than ever in history!

I sometimes get the sense that we spend too much time discussing minor differences that separate us instead of focusing on

the most remarkable similarities that make us family. I celebrate
that our theologians continue to have meetings and discussions.
Taking into account the context of the sacred Scriptures and the
discernment needed to address open-ended questions, there is
another level of ecumenism that calls us to move with greater
haste in our meetings: the ecumenism of charity, that of having
an outstretched hand to our neighbors. We have seen many
beautiful examples of this in the last years, such as when two
siblings commit themselves equally to the poor and do not ask if
they are Lutherans, Presbyterians, or Anglicans. I have had the
opportunity to witness this on my trips outside Italy, as I did in
April of 2016 when I went to the island of Lesbos, the embodi-
ment of the immigration drama, alongside Ecumenical Patriarch
Bartholomew I of Constantinople.

This is not ecumenism merely for show. Instead, I see it as an
essential attitude, a prism by which we can test the rest of our
lives as believers. I like to think that we have many faces of ecumenism: that of blood, that of charity, that of the poor, and that
of mission, which calls us to the streets. We must be a community of believers on the move, close to the weak and the young,
to whom we must bequeath this fraternal mission.

We are also called to open dialogue with nonbelievers. I like to
think of one of the great paintings by Raphael, *The School of Athens*. In this painting, Plato and Aristotle occupy the center of the
scene, observed and surrounded by classical masters of Greece
who represent Western thought and who make up the master-
piece. Both are walking and dialoguing side by side. Even though
it is a small gesture, neither one of them ever ceases to keep their
point of view: Plato points with his right hand toward the sky,
which is divine, while his left hand holds a copy of *Timaeus*. Aristotle points with his right hand to the Earth, the terrestrial, and
in his left hand he holds a volume of *Ethics*. Since the beginning
of my papacy, I have tried to encourage dialogue with nonbeliev-

ers based on open communication. However, we also must be the Church on the move.

In the same way that we are called to act quickly on a global level with our brothers and sisters of other Churches and with non-Christians, we should also involve those who do not claim any faith. For this reason, in two of my encyclical letters—*Laudato Si'* and *Fratelli Tutti*—I decided to touch on themes that affect all of humanity. These letters were written to all men and women of goodwill. As the Second Vatican Council teaches us, "The joys and the hopes, the griefs and the anxieties of the men of this age, especially those who are poor or in any way afflicted, these are the joys and hopes, the griefs and anxieties of the followers of Christ. Indeed, nothing genuinely human fails to raise an echo in their hearts."[7] In light of this, I wrote both of these encyclicals from my Christian heritage, to address those who do not consider themselves believers. I did this because all are part of the solution to the troubles that afflict us.

The grand challenges before us in our world today are not projects that are for "the few, or an enlightened or outspoken minority which claims to speak for everyone."[8] Rather, "it is about agreeing to live together, a social and cultural pact."[9]

In this sense, many initiatives seem to give some continuity and institutionalization to this dialogue. For example, the *Cortile dei Gentili* (the court of the gentiles) is a space for believers and nonbelievers to exchange ideas on the topics of ethics, art, science, and the search for transcendence. I encourage others to be developed also.

Often different groups of scientists come to the Vatican. These groups consist of believers, agnostics, and atheists, but they have a common goal of finding ways to build bridges, form agreements, and come up with generative proposals. This shows us that we do not need to be the same kind of people to commit ourselves to common causes.

Once we recognize this common place of belonging, it will be easier for us to face the different challenges that we have before us as human beings. As believers, we are called to collaborate with men and women of goodwill. Even if they do not profess any religion, we can come together to find practical answers for various issues such as violence, hunger, the misery that afflicts millions of people, the environmental crisis, and corruption. The younger generations demand us to initiate processes in which we search for solutions to end all types of violence, especially those perpetrated in the name of religion. They call us to be more like Abel and less like Cain.

One of the critical challenges we face as believers is unearthing any glimpse of violence that may arise between us and our brothers and sisters. I want to remind us that no religion is terroristic. There is no such thing as a Christian terrorist, a Jewish terrorist, or a Muslim terrorist. There are in all religions, as well as in all nations, fundamentalist and violent people who "with intolerant generalizations . . . become stronger because they feed on hate and xenophobia."[10]

It is essential to remind ourselves that "violence has no basis in our fundamental religious convictions, but only in their distortion."[11] The war in Ukraine has made us think once more about the positions of brothers and sisters who use religion as the justification for acts of hate and violence. There is no space for these types of expressions in the name of God.

At the same time, no religion is immune to the risk of fundamentalist or extremist deviations by individuals or groups.[12] We must overcome these pockets of prejudice, focus on the positive values that persist, and move forward to become sources of hope.

It is vital along these lines to warn against those who are tempted to distort the message, thinking they can shield themselves from God when they commit acts of violence and abuse.

No one should profess religion as the motive for their actions that go against human dignity and fundamental human rights.

The first objective of fraternity among believers and non-believers must be to work together to fight the actions of fundamentalism that feed off situations of injustice and instability—conditions that lead to wars.

The best antidote against fundamentalism is to work ceaselessly for true equality of opportunities: worthwhile jobs and conditions that make life develop holistically. With these goals in mind, we can fully integrate into our societies those who are different from us and those who have recently arrived.

In Europe, for example, there have been situations in which people use the name of God to commit violent acts. They were born in its large capitals as children of immigrants but have been relegated to poverty and stigmatization for having a different skin color or religion. These Europeans were born there and are legal citizens, but they have lived since childhood in a world that segregates them, whether through bullying in school or the extra difficulty of finding a job. This is not a justification; it is merely a sign that real and healthy integration can be the best antidote so that fundamentalism does not take hold in us.

Violence in the name of God is a betrayal of religion. Therefore, we must say no to any hate perpetrated in God's name or in the name of any other religion. I remember the declaration I made with my brother, the Grand Imam of Al-Azhar, Ahmed El-Tayeb:

Moreover, we resolutely declare that religions must never incite war, hateful attitudes, hostility and extremism, nor must they incite violence or the shedding of blood. These tragic realities are the consequence of a deviation from religious teachings. They result from a political manipulation of religions and from interpretations made by religious groups who, in the course of history, have taken advantage of the power of religious sentiment in the hearts of men and women in order to make them act in a way that has nothing to do with the truth of religion. This is done for the purpose of achieving objectives that are political, economic, worldly and short-sighted.[13]

Religions should not tolerate the deformations of our faith. We are committed to eradicating the evil of fundamentalism in our communities. However, we cannot do this alone; we need the involvement and decisions of those in political, economic, social, educational, and cultural spheres.

As religious leaders, we should never tire of repeating that we cannot kill in the name of God. However, we also want to shift our energies from this shared agenda and point to the urgent need before us: a population that is increasingly wealthier and, at the same time, more indifferent, even with its home, Earth.

I look back at the ecumenical meeting I had toward the end of 2021 with Ecumenical Patriarch Bartholomew I and Archbishop Justin Welby to sign the joint declaration in which we warn of the need for environmental sustainability, its impact on poverty, and the importance of global cooperation.

We are aware that we must leave the world in a better place than we found it.[14] This is true in regard to our caring for our Common Home, yes, but not just this. Given that most humans on Earth declare that they are believers, why do religions not take advantage of this reality, initiating a dialogue concerning the care of nature, the defense of the poor, and the construction of networks of respect and fraternity?

This dialogue must not exclude the defense of life in all its phases, just as the Grand Imam of Al-Azhar and I proposed in condemning practices "that are a threat to life such as genocide, acts of terrorism, forced displacement, human organ trafficking, abortion and euthanasia."[15] Like the Catholic faith teaches, we believe that life begins at conception and ends in natural death. Additionally, we ask all our brothers and sisters to join in the absolute rejection of the death penalty without any ambiguity.[16] In this call, we invite not only all Christians but also all brothers and sisters of other faith traditions and all men and women of goodwill.

The path of dialogue between religions has been central in the leadership of my predecessors, and I have proposed that it continue to be an imperative for us in facing the concrete challenges of the world. This dialogue is not something we can merely opt out of. Our encounters with the other cannot exclude those who do not consider themselves believers. Only if we walk together with men and women of goodwill can we respond to the evident globalization of indifference that seeks to make us enemies, creates the conditions for the proliferation of fundamentalism, and aims to take the lives of millions of people through war and poverty. Fraternity is the path forward. For this reason, I ask that the name of God not be used to incite acts of hate, war, and savagery; instead, I pray that God's presence will allow us to walk together.

Epilogue

"Pilgrims of Hope"

✝

During his brief papacy, the beatified John Paul I dedicated one of his four audiences to hope and called this virtue "obligatory for every Christian."[1] To this beautiful definition, I would like to add that the call to hope must transcend the parameters of just those who believe. It is a virtue that can be present in each man and woman of goodwill.

This is a difficult time to have faith, even though each day there is uplifting news. In my encyclical letter *Fratelli Tutti*, dedicated to universal fraternity, I stated, "God continues to sow abundant seeds of goodness in our human family. The recent pandemic enabled us to recognize and appreciate once more all those around us who, in the midst of fear, responded by putting their lives on the line."[2]

How many children came into this world during a time full of darkness and unrest! How many people grew closer than ever before, more strongly embraced the hope that this tempest would pass, or renewed their belief in the bonds of humanity that would overcome this time! A few years ago, an Anglican brother, Desmond Tutu of South Africa, shared a beautiful idea of how to look at the future. He said, "Hope is being able to see that there is light despite all of the darkness."[3]

We must turn our attention to something else: putting the pandemic behind us was not handled as it could have been. As we consider how to leave the pandemic behind, I always think that with a crisis, we leave it either better or worse, but never the same. Sadly, in many cases we see the resurgence of certain attitudes that existed before the pandemic. A recent report put together by a group of judges from Latin America and Africa shows a very discouraging fact: vaccines are "not available or accessible—in a universal form—for all of the world population, especially those people living on the African continent with a low level of vaccination."[4] I accept this diagnosis with great pain. This health emergency asked us to overcome specific thought patterns and to embrace the opportunity to give to those who have less.

Yet as we are trying to move beyond the pandemic, Ukraine's war drapes a dark cloak over the world once more, with Europe as its epicenter. So it is a new challenge to test our hope.

We are going backward after our many steps forward, which is not good, but it does not have to be definitive. Some have changed and grown. Some have a new vision of life, and some do not. This war is an example of this backward behavior. Once more, we descend into war. A war to test weapons and sell them.

For this reason, with these ten petitions in the name of God, I want to call all men and women of goodwill to accompany me in having hope for the world to come.

When I reflect on hope, I cannot help but think, first of all, of those deprived of their freedom. The incarcerated are living examples that we can welcome the presence and compassion of God, no matter what evil has been committed. There is no heart that the love of the Almighty cannot enter. It is precisely here in our hearts that hope takes root; from there, it illuminates our present—a present that can be disturbed and darkened due to all the situations that bring with them sadness and pain. Those who are incarcerated can't be sentenced without offering them a window of hope. God is tender toward them, so we should pray for them so that they may find a window of hope that offers them a way out toward a better life.

I always prefer to speak of hope and not optimism. Since optimism is a mood that today is here and tomorrow is gone, it is variable. Some are optimistic, others pessimistic, but this is not how to relate to the future. I am a Christian and like to say, "I have hope."

That is why in moments like these, amid everything that is happening in the world—including again facing the cruelty of war—it is essential to raise our voices of hope: it is the only voice that can challenge the status quo and get involved in the reality that surrounds us.

Hope, in general terms, encouraged me to select the theme for the next Jubilee, which will take place in 2025. "Pilgrims of hope" is an invitation to walk together.

Hope in a better world is the through line that connects these ten petitions in the name of God, which I have offered here and invited all of us to help realize. There are no magic formulas, yet specific postures can help us with our neighbors, Common Home, and many other issues. For example, we need to restore a sense of universal fraternity and not shield our eyes from the tragic circumstances of the poor that prevent men, women, and children from living with dignity.

This hope, different from optimism, never fails. An image by Bansky, a contemporary artist, on a wall in London illustrates this: we see a little girl letting a red balloon in the shape of a heart float away. Next to the image of the girl, highlighting the balloon, is a phrase written in black and white: "There is always hope."[5] This same hope "bids us live fully in the present."[6] This is definitely a gift that God wants to give all of us.

I make the petitions you are holding in your hand in the name of God, but I want to call into action believers and nonbelievers.

As in two of my encyclicals, I wanted to dialogue with all about our Common Home, universal fraternity, and the concerns of humanity.

I want to dedicate a special paragraph for all people of the Catholic faith to remind them that we need to be faithful people of God, mobilized together if we want to see some of the changes I plead for in this book. In my apostolic constitution *Praedicate Evangelium,* I recently issued a call for missionary mobilization in the entire Church. The pope and his collaborators "know that they were not established by Christ to undertake by themselves the entire saving mission of the Church to the world."[7] This is a call for all to walk together in hope since we will go nowhere without hope.

After hope, mercy must follow. Mercy was the subject of the Extraordinary Jubilee of 2015 to 2016. At that moment, I wanted to bring attention to the fact that we have been shown mercy and that the mercy of God is beyond our own limits, sins, and errors. There is a story of Saint John Marie Vianney, the "Priest of Ars": A widow was crying for her husband, who had committed suicide by jumping off a bridge into the Seine. "He is now in hell," she said. The priest told her that the mercy of God was so great that it was found between the bridge and the river.

Mercy is a subject that I touch on often. We are all redeemed by mercy. In my office in Saint Martha's House, there is an image of the capital on a column at the Basilica of Saint Mary Magdalene in Vézelay Abbey. In the medieval period, when there were very few literate people, the capitals atop these columns served as catechisms. People would look up to them and understand. This capital shows Judas Iscariot hanged, and below him is the devil, who throws him into hell. On the other side of the capital is the Good Shepherd rescuing Judas with a sly smile. This capital is a whole catechesis teaching that the mercy of God is stronger than anything.

One of the fruits of the Extraordinary Jubilee was the creation of the Missionaries of Mercy, who play an essential role in penitential doctrine and the ministry of the Sacrament of Reconciliation. They also go to places where the presence of Catholics is limited, traveling long distances to visit different communities. Before the Extraordinary Jubilee, not all priests had permission to absolve the crime of abortion, for example. When a woman went to Reconciliation because of this sin, she would be told to come the next day because the priest had to ask permission from his bishop. Now all priests can absolve the grave sin of abortion.[8] Other grave sins must go through the Apostolic Penitentiary, yet these missionaries can also intervene. They let people know that they will be in a city; then people come, and they listen. It is a way to allow people to experience God's mercy concretely. Right there, where they are.

In this sense, I confess every fifteen days with a Franciscan. In confession I experience God's forgiveness, and this helps me to have hope. And hope is not something static but something in motion, allowing us to move forward. A beautiful image is that of the anchor, which appears in the Bible: we throw the anchor over, which holds us to a place, and we walk toward that place.

Let us be the "pilgrims of hope" moving toward the future. I have presented here ten petitions I make in the name of God, but we all need to mobilize together. All the missteps we have taken and successes we have achieved must be lessons we learn from, since the road is not easy. Let us be reminded, "That is why no one is saved alone, as an isolated individual. Rather, God draws us to himself, taking into account the complex fabric of interpersonal relationships present in a human community. God wanted to enter into the life and history of a people."[9]

As human beings, we need to remember our history, have the courage to face the present, and have hope to go into the future. The past should not be forgotten: that of our family, that of our nation, that of ourselves. Courage is necessary because if we do not have courage today, we cannot walk forward. But this is not an act of isolated or individual courage. It is the courage to know that we are accompanied and sustained by others. This also gives us hope and the courage to trust others and walk onward.

There is a tango song that is almost one hundred years old and, unfortunately, is still very relevant. In 1934, this song described the twentieth century as an "unfolding of insolent evil." It is our job to ensure that the twenty-first century is not the same or worse. We should not have the attitude of "come on, let's go, it's all gonna be the same anyways."[10] Let us ask God to give us hope for a better future.

In this sense, I am reminded of a passage from my first audience after being elected as pope that attests to what it means to be a pilgrim and mobilize forward with hope: "Following Jesus means learning to come out of ourselves . . . in order to go to meet others, to go towards the outskirts of existence, to be the first to take a step towards our brothers and our sisters, especially those who are the most distant, those who are forgotten, those who are most in need of understanding, comfort and help."[11]

I want to share with you the words of the first African Nobel laureate, Albert Lutuli, who, after accepting the award in 1961, said, "May the day come soon, when the people of the world will rouse themselves, and together effectively stamp out any threat to peace in whatever quarter of the world it may be found. When that day comes, there shall be 'peace on earth and goodwill amongst men,' as was announced by the Angels when that great messenger of peace, Our Lord came to earth."[12] With hope, knowing that I am accompanied by all you fellow pilgrims in the desire for peace, I ask this especially in the name of God.

Postscript of the Editor

By Hernán Reyes Alcaide

The idea for this book came during a speech by Pope Francis to the Popular Movements on October 16, 2021, in which he thanked these groups of "social poets" for helping the neediest during the pandemic. Although the Covid-19 emergency had already been going on for over a year and a half, the pontiff used the Beatitudes as the foundation to prescribe the world coming together and called us to build a new reality. All of humanity was undergoing a new reality based on this disruptive experience. The pope invited all peoples, institutions, and organizations to take measures to stop the current system, which he called an "out-of-control locomotive hurtling towards the abyss."

With the historical anchoring of the Social Doctrine of the Church, read through the experience of the pandemic, Francis spoke bluntly about nine key issues that urgently needed (and still need) to change course if we want to truly "dream of a new world together."[1] Since then, he has held to these axes to try to help humanity end up better than we were before the pandemic. As he posed in his monumental *Urbi et Orbi* of March 27, 2020, the pandemic is a crisis we can emerge from either better or worse, but never the same.

I proposed to him the idea of developing further the format of these petitions "in the name of God" and giving them a broader reach to all men and women of goodwill—taking up again what is synthesized in the first few paragraphs of the encyclical *Laudato Si'*: "to every person living on this planet."[2]

The first proposal Francis accepted was a text that would take up the pleas of the October 2021 speech and that would develop each point alongside the thoughts of his predecessors and the Social Doctrine of the Church.

We were not going to do a formal interview with questions and answers; that was clear from the beginning. Instead, the process would require that I participate more broadly and profoundly in the editing of the text based on his suggestions and reading recommendations given in personal exchanges over the telephone and email.

As the project was developing, it became more and more evident that the tenth anniversary of this papacy obliged us to incorporate topics that had not originally been included in the petitions "in the name of God" in 2021. Therefore, we included particular issues that helped convert the text into a more holistic outlook, covering issues beyond those of his first decade as pope. As the subtitle suggests, this outlook laid out the challenges that Francis proposed need to be addressed for the world to have a future of hope: the fight against sexual abuse, the abuse of power, and the abuse of conscience. We also included the evolution of the doctrine of the Church in its rejection of the death penalty and its promotion of the role of women in society, which are just some of the themes we decided on.

Additionally, the eruption of the war in Ukraine was an important reminder to include a strong plea against any further escalation and justification of war, just as the pope emphasized on his trip to Canada in July of 2022: "How much we need to listen to and dialogue with one another in order to step back from . . . widespread aggressiveness and the temptation to divide the world into good people and bad!"[3]

The first step was to get the plan configured and to review speeches, messages, and comments from 2013 onward to identify the central concepts that the pope had spoken about for each theme. Afterward, as we worked together he was developing new ideas in addition to those original nine petitions and then returned to propose ten of the big themes of his papacy.

One of the challenges was to achieve a certain musicality that would imitate a conversation each reader of this book could have with the pope without losing the collective dimension of these calls to work toward a future of hope.

The pope thus presents a book encompassing the significant issues of his papacy, with his ideas supported by statistics and his voice enriched by the works of artists and thinkers as varied as Dante, Virgil, Gabriela Mistral, and Jorge Luis Borges. In this book, he reveals precise knowledge about the modes of communication and the vernacular of the second decade of the twenty-first century. This text does not exclude references to TikTok or the dangers of the internet age. He also confirms his conceptual continuity with his predecessors, whom he takes as his starting point for analyzing these ten petitions. Yet, in a world that is becoming increasingly complex—even as we worked on this project—Francis looks to the future and proposes to live with hope in the years to come.

There is a quote by Austrian composer Gustav Mahler that the pope looks to both in public and private to give a sense of a movement that he sees as ideal. It is an ideal that holds all the traditions, doctrines, and customs in the Church and in humanity moving forward: "Tradition is the guarantee of the future and not the container of the ashes."[4] This is a quote that he reminded his listeners of on his trip to Canada at the end of July 2022. It reflects the constant and fruitful dialogue that the pope wants to have between the past and the present. The connection between the past and the present is personified in the relationship between the elderly and young people. This is another of the topics that permeates the whole book.

Within the framework of a third world war, which we see beginning part by part, the eyes of the pope are focused forward and filled with hope. Without any doubt or hesitation, Pope Francis is confident in affirming that "there is still time"[5] to make the necessary changes to help us build a future of hope.

The devastated environment, an unbridled market-centered economy, a political situation increasingly removed from the common good, and systems of health that decreasingly take care of those most fragile in society are all problems the pope speaks about in this book. The common thread of all these problems is that humans can rectify them since they were caused by humans. This is why Pope Francis has hope for the future. And this is why the book ends with a call to courage.

The French anthropologist Didier Fassin proposed in his recent work, "If the world can be otherwise—and by the way, it already has in the past and in other places—then change is always possible and feeds our hopes."[6] For the concrete themes presented here, it is ultimately in the hope that this change could be possible that the pope makes these ten petitions in the name of God with humility and openness.

The original draft of this book was written by Pope Francis in Spanish. The meticulous work that Giuseppe Romano did for the Italian translation gives readers a text that is a faithful version of the original text. In Buenos Aires, Ana Clara Pérez Cotten was the "first reader," contributing knowledge, precision, and order: to her, thank you.

I want to thank the team at Piemme: Antonella Bonamici, who welcomed the project from the beginning and suggested ideas to enrich it, and Cecilia Mastrogiovanni, for the continued work of editing, giving it a fresh and modern look.

Notes

✝

Introduction

1. Bertrand Russell, *Mortals and Others, Volume II: American Essays, 1931–1935* (London; New York: Routledge, 1998), 318.
2. Andrea Camilleri, *Háblame de ti: Carta a Matilda* (Barcelona: Salamandra, 2020), 115–16.
3. Rainer Maria Rilke, "Wendung," Die Gedichte von Rainer Maria Rilke, rainer-maria-rilke.de/100138wendung.html.

Chapter 1

1. Pope Francis, "Meeting 'The Protection of Minors in the Church': Address of His Holiness at the End of the Eucharistic Concelebration (24 February 2019)," www.vatican.va/content/francesco/en/speeches/2019/february/documents/papa-francesco_20190224_incontro-protezioneminori-chiusura.html.
2. Pope Francis, "To Members of the 'Meter' Association (15 May 2021)," www.vatican.va/content/francesco/en/speeches/2021/may/documents/papa-francesco_20210515_associazione-meter.html.
3. Pope Francis, "Meeting 'The Protection of Minors in the Church': Address of His Holiness at the End of the Eucharistic Concelebration (24 February 2019)."
4. Pope Francis, "Apostolic Constitution 'Pascite Gregem Dei' of the Holy Father Francis, Reforming Book VI of the

Code of Canon Law (1 June 2021)," press.vatican.va/
content/salastampa/en/bollettino/pubblico/2021/06/01/
210601c.html.

5. Pope Francis, "To Members of the 'Meter' Association
(15 May 2021)."

6. Pope Francis, "Apostolic Journey to Canada: Vespers with
Bishops, Priests, Deacons, Consecrated Persons, Seminarians and Pastoral Workers in the Cathedral of Notre
Dame. Homily of His Holiness (28 July 2022)," www
.vatican.va/content/francesco/en/homilies/2022/
documents/20220728-omelia-vespri-quebec.html.

Chapter 2

1. Pope Francis, "Video Message of the Holy Father on the
Occasion of the Fourth World Meeting of Popular Movements (EMMP) (16 October 2021)," www.vatican.va/
content/francesco/en/messages/pont-messages/2021/
documents/20211016-videomessaggio-movimenti
popolari.html.

2. Pope Francis, "Laudato Si' (24 May 2015)," www.vatican
.va/content/francesco/en/encyclicals/documents/papa
-francesco_20150524_enciclica-laudato-si.html.

3. "Compendium of the Social Doctrine of the Church," 466,
www.vatican.va/roman_curia/pontifical_councils/
justpeace/documents/rc_pc_justpeace_doc_20060526
_compendio-dott-soc_en.html.

4. "Compendium of the Social Doctrine of the Church," 460.

5. "Final Document of the Synod of Bishops. The Amazon:
New Paths for the Church and for an Integral Ecology
(26 October 2019)," www.vatican.va/roman_curia/synod/
documents/rc_synod_doc_20191026_sinodo-amazzonia
_en.html.

6. Pope Paul VI, "Octogesima Adveniens (14 May 1971),"
21, www.vatican.va/content/paul-vi/en/apost_letters/
documents/hf_p-vi_apl_19710514_octogesima-adveniens
.html.

7. Pope Benedict XVI, "To the Diplomatic Corps Accredited to the Holy See for the Traditional Exchange of New Year Greetings (8 January 2007)," www.vatican.va/content/benedict-xvi/en/speeches/2007/january/documents/hf_ben-xvi_spe_20070108_diplomatic-corps.html.

8. "Compendium of the Social Doctrine of the Church," 463.

9. Pope Francis, "Laudato Si' (24 May 2015)," 60.

10. Ibid.

11. Ibid., 135.

12. Ibid., 139.

13. "Final Document of the Synod of Bishops. The Amazon: New Paths for the Church and for an Integral Ecology (26 October 2019)," 12.

14. Pope Francis, "Video Message of the Holy Father on the Occasion of the Fourth World Meeting of Popular Movements (EMMP) (16 October 2021)," 2.

15. Pope Francis, "Laudato Si' (24 May 2015)," 145.

Chapter 3

1. Miguel de Cervantes and Henry Edward Watts, *Don Quixote Of La Mancha*, vol. III, Ch. 16 (London: Adam and Charles Black, 1895).

2. Pope Francis, "Gaudete et Exsultate: Apostolic Exhortation on the Call to Holiness in Today's World (19 March 2018)," 6, www.vatican.va/content/francesco/en/apost_exhortations/documents/papa-francesco_esortazione-ap_20180319_gaudete-et-exsultate.html.

3. Fyodor Dostoevsky, *Crime and Punishment: A Novel in Six Parts with Epilogue*, trans. Richard Pevear and Larissa Volokhonsky, Vintage Classics (New York: Vintage Books, 1993), 425.

4. Pope Francis, "Homily at Casa Santa Marta" (18 June 2018).

5. Ibid.

6. Pope Francis, "Homily at Casa Santa Marta" (17 May 2018).

7. Pope Francis and Austen Ivereigh, *Let Us Dream: The Path to a Better Future* (New York: Simon & Schuster, 2020), 28.

8. Pope Francis, "To the Participants in the Congress on 'Child Dignity in the Digital World' (6 October 2017)," www.vatican.va/content/francesco/en/speeches/2017/october/documents/papa-francesco_20171006_congresso-childdignity-digitalworld.html.

Chapter 4

1. Pope Francis, "Fratelli Tutti (3 October 2020)," 176, www.vatican.va/content/francesco/en/encyclicals/documents/papa-francesco_20201003_enciclica-fratelli-tutti.html.

2. Pope Francis, "Apostolic Journey to Cyprus and Greece: Meeting with Authorities, Civil Society and the Diplomatic Corps (4 December 2021)," www.vatican.va/content/francesco/en/speeches/2021/december/documents/20211204-grecia-autorita.html.

3. Pope Francis, "Evangelii Gaudium: Apostolic Exhortation on the Proclamation of the Gospel in Today's World (24 November 2013)," 205, www.vatican.va/content/francesco/en/apost_exhortations/documents/papa-francesco_esortazione-ap_20131124_evangelii-gaudium.html.

4. "Compendium of the Social Doctrine of the Church," 164.

5. Ibid., 168.

6. "Catechism of the Catholic Church," 1910, www.vatican.va/archive/ENG0015/__P6K.HTM.

7. Pope Francis, "Fratelli Tutti (3 October 2020)," 176.

8. Ibid., 180.

9. Pope Paul VI, "Ecclesiam Suam (6 August 1964)," 38, www.vatican.va/content/paul-vi/en/encyclicals/documents/hf_p-vi_enc_06081964_ecclesiam.html.

10. Ibid., 81.

11. Pope Francis, "To the Diplomatic Corps Accredited to the Holy See for the Traditional Exchange of New Year Greetings (9 January 2020)," www.vatican.va/content/ francesco/en/speeches/2020/january/documents/papa -francesco_20200109_corpo-diplomatico.html.

12. Pope Francis, "Sixth World Day of the Poor (13 November 2022)," www.vatican.va/content/francesco/en/messages/ poveri/documents/20220613-messaggio-vi -giornatamondiale-poveri-2022.html.

13. Pope Leo XIII, "Rerum Novarum (15 May 1891)," www .vatican.va/content/leo-xiii/en/encyclicals/documents/hf _l-xiii_enc_15051891_rerum-novarum.html; Pope Pius XI, "Quadragesimo Anno (15 May 1931)," www.vatican .va/content/pius-xi/en/encyclicals/documents/hf_p-xi _enc_19310515_quadragesimo-anno.html; Pope Paul VI, "Regina Coeli Address Pentecost Sunday (17 May 1970)."

14. Pope Francis, "Video Message of the Holy Father on the Occasion of the Fourth World Meeting of Popular Movements (EMMP) (16 October 2021)."

15. Pope Francis, "Evangelii Gaudium: Apostolic Exhortation on the Proclamation of the Gospel in Today's World (24 November 2013)," 218.

16. Dante Alighieri, "Inferno 3—Digital Dante," trans. Allen Mandelbaum, 50, digitaldante.columbia.edu/dante/divine -comedy/inferno/inferno-3/.

17. Dostoevsky, *Crime and Punishment*.

Chapter 5

1. Virgil, *Vergil's Aeneid: The Aeneid: An Epic Poem of Rome*, trans. L. R. Lind, vol. XI (Bloomington: Indiana University Press, 1963), 362.

2. "Compendium of the Social Doctrine of the Church," 497.

3. Pope Pius XII, "Radiomensaje En El Alba y En La Luz (24 December 1941)," www.vatican.va/content/pius

-xii/es/speeches/1941/documents/hf_p-xii_spe
_19411224_radiomessage-peace.html.

4. Pope Francis, "Fratelli Tutti (3 October 2020)," 256.

5. Elie Wiesel, *And the Sea Is Never Full: Memoirs, 1969–* (New York: Knopf Doubleday, 2000), 403.

6. Stockholm International Peace Research Institute, "SIPRI Yearbook 2021: Armaments, Disarmament and International Security" (Stockholm, 2021), sipri.org/sites/default/files/2021-06/sipri_yb21_summary_en_v2_0.pdf.

7. Pope Francis, "Apostolic Journey. . .Meeting with the Members of the General Assembly of the United Nations Organization (25 September 2015)," www.vatican.va/content/francesco/en/speeches/2015/september/documents/papa-francesco_20150925_onu-visita.html.

8. Pope Francis, "Fratelli Tutti (3 October 2020)," 173.

9. Pope Francis, "Apostolic Journey to Kazakhstan: Meeting with the Authorities, Civil Society and the Diplomatic Corps (13 September 2022)" www.vatican.va/content/francesco/en/speeches/2022/september/documents/20220913-kazakhstan-autorita.html.

10. Pope Francis, "Laudato Si' (24 May 2015)," 137.

11. Pope Francis, "Apostolic Journey to Kazakhstan."

12. Pope Francis, "Laudato Si' (24 May 2015)," 104.

13. Pope Francis, "LIII World Day of Peace 2020—Peace as a Journey of Hope: Dialogue, Reconciliation and Ecological Conversion (1 January 2020)," www.vatican.va/content/francesco/en/messages/peace/documents/papa-francesco_20191208_messaggio-53giornatamondiale-pace2020.html.

14. Pope Paul VI, "Visit to the United Nations: Speech to the United Nations Organization (4 October 1965)," www.vatican.va/content/paul-vi/en/speeches/1965/documents/hf_p-vi_spe_19651004_united-nations.html.

15. Pope Francis, "Apostolic Journey to Japan: Address on Nuclear Weapons at the Atomic Bomb Hypocenter Park (24 November 2019)," www.vatican.va/content/francesco/

en/speeches/2019/november/documents/papa-francesco
_20191124_messaggio-arminucleari-nagasaki.html.

16. Martin Luther King, Jr., "Pilgrimage to Nonviolence," The
Martin Luther King, Jr., Research and Education Institute,
28 July 2014, kinginstitute.stanford.edu/king-papers/
documents/pilgrimage-nonviolence.

Chapter 6

1. Pope Francis, "Apostolic Journey to Cyprus and Greece:
Visit to the Refugees at 'Reception and Identification Centre' in Mytilene (5 December 2021)," www.vatican.va/
content/francesco/en/speeches/2021/december/
documents/20211205-grecia-rifugiati.html.

2. Faena Aleph, "Octavio Paz Revealed the Meaning of Life
in This Poem," faena.com/aleph/octavio-paz-revealed-the
-meaning-of-life-in-this-poem.

3. Jorge Luis Borges, *Historia de la eternidad* (Madrid: Alianza
Editorial, 1971).

4. Pope Francis, "Message for the 106th World Day of Migrants and Refugees, 2020 (27 September 2020)," www
.vatican.va/content/francesco/en/messages/migration/
documents/papa-francesco_20200513_world-migrants
-day-2020.html.

5. For the full report, see Internal Displacement Monitoring
Centre, "2020 Global Report on Internal Displacement,"
IDMC, internal-displacement.org/sites/default/files/
publications/documents/2020-IDMC-GRID-executive
-summary.pdf.

Chapter 7

1. Pope Paul VI, "Messages of the Council: To Women
(8 December 1965)," www.vatican.va/content/paul-vi/en/
speeches/1965/documents/hf_p-vi_spe_19651208
_epilogo-concilio-donne.html.

2. Pope Francis and Ivereigh, *Let Us Dream*, 62.

3. Pope Francis, "Apostolic Journey to Canada: Participation in the 'Lac Ste. Anne Pilgrimage' and Liturgy of the Word (26 July 2022)," www.vatican.va/content/francesco/en/ homilies/2022/documents/20220726-omelia-lacsteanne -canada.html.

4. For full interview, see Pope Francis, "Press Conference of the Holy Father during the Flight Back (28 July 2013)," www.vatican.va/content/francesco/en/speeches/2013/ july/documents/papa-francesco_20130728_gmg -conferenza-stampa.html.

5. Pope Francis, "Fratelli Tutti (3 October 2020)," 23.

6. "Infographic | A Global Look at Femicide," Wilson Center, 8 December 2021, wilsoncenter.org/article/ infographic-global-look-femicide.

7. Data from "Female Genital Mutilation," World Health Organization, who.int/health-topics/female-genital -mutilation.

8. Pope John Paul II, "Familiaris Consortio (22 November 1981)," 45, www.vatican.va/content/john-paul-ii/en/ apost_exhortations/documents/hf_jp-ii_exh_19811122 _familiaris-consortio.html.

9. Pope Francis and Domenico Agasso, "Pope Francis: 'We must save lives, not build weapons to destroy them'," Vatican News, 14 March 2021, www.vaticannews .va/en/pope/news/2021-03/pope-francis-book-excerpt -god-world-to-come.html.

10. "Compendium of the Social Doctrine of the Church," 295.

Chapter 8

1. Jo Walker et al., "The 2022 Commitment to Reducing Inequality Index, Development Finance International, Oxfam, 11 October 2022, 34, doi.org/10.21201/2022 .9325.

2. Joe Myers, "These Charts Show the Growing Gap between the World's Richest and Poorest," World Economic Forum, 10 December 2021, weforum.org/agenda/2021/12/global-income-inequality-gap-report-rich-poor/.

3. Pope Francis, "Evangelii Gaudium: Apostolic Exhortation on the Proclamation of the Gospel in Today's World (24 November 2013)," 53.

4. Ibid., 54.

5. UN Children's Fund (UNICEF), "Progress for Children Beyond Averages: Learning from the MDGs," UNICEF, 22 June 2015, 26, unicef.org/media/50866/file/Progress _for_Children_No._11-ENG.pdf.

6. Congregation for the Doctrine of the Faith and The Dicastery for Promoting Integral Human Development, " 'Oeconomicae et Pecuniariae Quaestiones'. Considerations for an Ethical Discernment Regarding Some Aspects of the Present Economic-Financial System of the Congregation for the Doctrine of the Faith and the Dicastery for Promoting Integral Human Development (17 May 2018)," 1, press.vatican.va/content/salastampa/en/bollettino/pubblico/2018/05/17/180517a.html.

7. Pope John Paul II, "Sollicitudo Rei Socialis (30 December 1987)," 40, www.vatican.va/content/john-paul-ii/en/encyclicals/documents/hf_jp-ii_enc_30121987_sollicitudo-rei-socialis.html.

8. Pope John Paul II, "Centesimus Annus (1 May 1991)," 35, www.vatican.va/content/john-paul-ii/en/encyclicals/documents/hf_jp-ii_enc_01051991_centesimus-annus.html.

9. Congregation for the Doctrine of the Faith and The Dicastery for Promoting Integral Human Development, " 'Oeconomicae et Pecuniariae Quaestiones' (17 May 2018)," 32.

10. "Compendium of the Social Doctrine of the Church," 171; 178.

11. Pope Paul VI, "To the World Land Reform Conference (27 June 1966)," www.vatican.va/content/paul-vi/en/

speeches/1966/documents/hf_p-vi_spe_19660627
_riforma-agraria.html.

12. Pope Francis, "Evangelii Gaudium: Apostolic Exhortation
on the Proclamation of the Gospel in Today's World
(24 November 2013)," 71.

13. Pope Francis, "Fratelli Tutti (3 October 2020)," 119.

14. Ibid.

15. Italo Calvino, "Italo Calvino on 'Invisible Cities,'" *Columbia: A Journal of Literature and Art*, no. 8 (1983), 41.

16. "Compendium of the Social Doctrine of the Church," 177.

17. Pope Francis, "Fratelli Tutti (3 October 2020)," 162.

18. FAO et al., *The State of Food Security and Nutrition in the World 2022. Repurposing Food and Agricultural Policies to Make Healthy Diets More Affordable* (Rome: FAO, 2022), 13, doi
.org/10.4060/cc0639en.

19. For more information, see UNICEF, "Global Hunger Crisis Pushing One Child into Severe Malnutrition Every Minute in 15 Crisis-Hit Countries," unicef.org/press
-releases/global-hunger-crisis-pushing-one-child-severe
-malnutrition-every-minute-15-crisis.

Chapter 9

1. Pope Francis, "LIV World Day of Peace 2021—A Culture of Care as a Path to Peace (1 January 2021)," www.vatican
.va/content/francesco/en/messages/peace/documents/
papa-francesco_20201208_messaggio-54giornatamondiale
-pace2021.html.

2. Pope Francis, "Moment of Prayer and 'Urbi et Orbi' Blessing Presided over by Pope Francis (27 March 2020)," www
.vatican.va/content/francesco/en/homilies/2020/
documents/papa-francesco_20200327_omelia-epidemia
.html.

3. For original video, see Devin Watkins and Pope Francis,
"Pope Francis Urges People to Get Vaccinated against
Covid-19," Vatican News, 18 August 2021, www

.vaticannews.va/en/pope/news/2021-08/pope-francis
-appeal-covid-19-vaccines-act-of-love.html.

4. Translated from the Spanish text, Papa Francisco, "Video-
mensaje Del Santo Padre a Los Participantes En El Semi-
nario Virtual 'América Latina: Iglesia, Papa Francisco y
Escenarios de La Pandemia' (19 November 2020)," www
.vatican.va/content/francesco/es/messages/pont
-messages/2020/documents/papa-francesco_20201119
_videomessaggio-americalatina.html.

5. Translated from the Spanish text, Papa Francisco, "A Los
Participantes En Un Encuentro Organizado Por La Comis-
ión Caridad y Salud de La Conferencia Episcopal Italiana
(10 February 2017)," www.vatican.va/content/francesco/
es/speeches/2017/february/documents/papa-francesco
_20170210_commissione-carita-salute.html.

6. Ibid.

7. Translated from the Spanish text, René Favaloro (Conferencia internacional sobre la salud del corazón en los
países en desarrollo. Una agenda para la acción para el
siglo XXI, New Delhi, 1999), fundacionfavaloro.org/
pensamientos/.

8. G. K. Chesterton, *The Man Who Was Thursday: A Nightmare*
(New York: Random House, 2001), 12.

9. Pope Francis, "Evangelii Gaudium: Apostolic Exhortation
on the Proclamation of the Gospel in Today's World
(24 November 2013)," 202.

10. Pope Francis, "General Audience of (9 February
2022)—Catechesis on Saint Joseph: 11. Saint Joseph, Patron of Good Death," www.vatican.va/content/francesco/
en/audiences/2022/documents/20220209-udienza
-generale.html.

11. Translated from the Spanish text, Papa Francisco,
"Oración del Papa Francisco por una respuesta cristiana a
los retos de la bioética," Comunidades Hispanas Ignaci-
anas, 11 March 2022, comunidadesignacianas.org/
reflexiones/031122.

12. Pope Francis, "Laudato Si' (24 May 2015)," 105.

13. Ibid.

14. Pope Francis, "General Audience of (23 February 2022)—Catechesis on Old Age: 1. The Grace of Time and the Bond between Age and Life," www.vatican .va/content/francesco/en/audiences/2022/documents/ 20220223-udienza-generale.html.

15. Pope Francis and Ivereigh, *Let Us Dream*, 58.

Chapter 10

1. Translated from the Spanish text, Papa Pablo VI, "Nostra Aetate," www.vatican.va/archive/hist_councils/ii_vatican _council/documents/vat-ii_decl_19651028_nostra-aetate _sp.html.

2. Pope Francis, "Apostolic Journey to the United Arab Emirates: Interreligious Meeting at the Founder's Memorial (4 February 2019)," www.vatican.va/content/francesco/ en/speeches/2019/february/documents/papa-francesco _20190204_emiratiarabi-incontrointerreligioso.html.

3. Ibid.

4. Pope Francis, "Video Message of His Holiness Pope Francis to Mark the Second International Day of Human Fraternity (4 February 2022)," www.vatican.va/content/ francesco/en/messages/pont-messages/2022/documents/ 20220204-videomessaggio-fratellanzaumana.html.

5. Jennifer Harper, "84 Percent of the World Population Has Faith; A Third Are Christian," *The Washington Times*, 23 December 2012, washingtontimes.com/blog/ watercooler/2012/dec/23/84-percent-world-population -has-faith-third-are-ch/.

6. Pope Francis, "Apostolic Journey to Egypt: To the Participants in the International Peace Conference (28 April 2017)," www.vatican.va/content/francesco/en/speeches/ 2017/april/documents/papa-francesco_20170428_egitto -conferenza-pace.html.

7. Pope Paul VI, "Gaudium et Spes," 1, www.vatican.va/archive/hist_councils/ii_vatican_council/documents/vat-ii_const_19651207_gaudium-et-spes_en.html.

8. Pope Francis, "Evangelii Gaudium: Apostolic Exhortation on the Proclamation of the Gospel in Today's World (24 November 2013)," 239.

9. Ibid.

10. Pope Francis, "Message of the Holy Father on the Occasion of the World Meetings of Popular Movements in Modesto (10 February 2017)," www.vatican.va/content/francesco/en/messages/pont-messages/2017/documents/papa-francesco_20170210_movimenti-popolari-modesto.html.

11. Pope Francis, "Fratelli Tutti (3 October 2020)," 282.

12. Pope Francis, "Apostolic Journey—United States of America: Visit to the Congress of the United States of America (24 September 2015)," www.vatican.va/content/francesco/en/speeches/2015/september/documents/papa-francesco_20150924_usa-us-congress.html.

13. Pope Francis, "Document on 'Human Fraternity for World Peace and Living Together' Signed by His Holiness Pope Francis and the Grand Imam of Al-Azhar Ahamad al-Tayyib (4 February 2019)" www.vatican.va/content/francesco/en/travels/2019/outside/documents/papa-francesco_20190204_documento-fratellanza-umana.html.

14. Pope Francis, "Laudato Si' (24 May 2015)," 194.

15. Pope Francis, "Document on 'Human Fraternity for World Peace and Living Together' Signed by His Holiness Pope Francis and the Grand Imam of Al-Azhar Ahamad al-Tayyib (4 February 2019)."

16. Pope Francis, "Fratelli Tutti (3 October 2020)," 263.

Epilogue

1. Pope John Paul I, "General Audience of 20 September 1978," www.vatican.va/content/john-paul-i/en/audiences/documents/hf_jp-i_aud_20091978.html.

2. Pope Francis, "Fratelli Tutti (3 October 2020)," 54.

3. Charlayne Hunter-Gault, "Remembering Desmond Tutu's Hope," *The New Yorker*, 27 December 2021, newyorker.com/news/postscript/remembering-desmond-tutus-hope.

4. Translated from the Spanish text, "Jueces de América y África urgen que se aseguren las vacunas para todos," Vatican News, 8 June 2022, www.vaticannews.va/es/mundo/news/2022-06/jueces-juezas-comites-panamericano-panafricano-vacunas-africa.html.

5. For more on the installation, see Banksy Explained, "Girl with Balloon: From Graffiti to Art History Icon," banksyexplained.com/issue/girl-with-balloon-graffiti-legend/.

6. Pope Francis, "Amoris Laetitia: Post-Synodal Apostolic Exhortation on Love in the Family (19 March 2016)," 219, www.vatican.va/content/francesco/en/apost_exhortations/documents/papa-francesco_esortazione-ap_20160319_amoris-laetitia.html.

7. Pope Francis, " 'Praedicate Evangelium' on the Roman Curia and Its Service to the Church and to the World (19 March 2022)," 10, www.vatican.va/content/francesco/en/apost_constitutions/documents/20220319-costituzione-ap-praedicate-evangelium.html#_ftn19.

8. Pope Francis, "Apostolic Letter Misericordia et Misera (20 November 2016)," www.vatican.va/content/francesco/en/apost_letters/documents/papa-francesco-lettera-ap_20161120_misericordia-et-misera.html.

9. Pope Francis, "Gaudete et Exsultate: Apostolic Exhortation on the Call to Holiness in Today's World (19 March 2018)," 6.

10. Translated from Spanish, Enrique Santos Discépolo, "Cambalache," Letras, letras.mus.br/enrique-santos -discepolo/345435/.

11. Pope Francis, "General Audience of 27 March 2013," www .vatican.va/content/francesco/en/audiences/2013/ documents/papa-francesco_20130327_udienza-generale .html.

12. Albert Lutuli, "The Nobel Peace Prize 1960," The Nobel Prize, nobelprize.org/prizes/peace/1960/lutuli/ acceptance-speech/.

Postscript of the Editor

1. Pope Francis, "Video Message of the Holy Father on the Occasion of the Fourth World Meeting of Popular Movements (EMMP) (16 October 2021)."

2. Pope Francis, "Laudato Si' (24 May 2015)," 3.

3. Pope Francis, "Apostolic Journey to Canada: Meeting with Civil Authorities, Representatives of Indigenous Peoples and Members of the Diplomatic Corps at the 'Citadelle de Québec' (27 July 2022)," www.vatican.va/content/ francesco/en/speeches/2022/july/documents/20220727 -autorita-canada.html.

4. Joshua J. Mcelwee, "Francis Criticizes Traditionalist Catholics Who 'Safeguard the Ashes' of the Past," National Catholic Reporter, ncronline.org/vatican/francis-criticizes -traditionalist-catholics-who-safeguard-ashes-past.

5. Pope Francis, "Video Message of the Holy Father on the Occasion of the Fourth World Meeting of Popular Movements (EMMP)," 2.

6. Translated from the Spanish text, Didier Fassin, *¿Cuánto vale una vida? o cómo pensar la dignidad humana en un mundo desigual* (Buenos Aires: Siglo Veintiuno Editores, 2022), 64, sigloxxieditores.com.ar/libro/cuanto-vale-una-vida/.

About the Author

POPE FRANCIS is the first Latin American to be elected to the chair of Peter. Born Jorge Mario Bergoglio in Buenos Aires, Argentina, he was ordained as a priest in 1969. He served as head of the Society of Jesus in Argentina from 1973 to 1979. In 1998 he became the archbishop of Buenos Aires, and in 2001 a cardinal. Following the resignation of his predecessor, Pope Benedict XVI, on February 28, 2013, the conclave elected Bergoglio, who chose the papal name Francis in honor of Saint Francis of Assisi.

HERNÁN REYES ALCAIDE is a correspondent in Rome for the Argentine news agency Télam. In 2017 he published *Latinoamérica*, a book-length interview with Pope Francis, the first from any Latin American journalist. In addition, he has worked with Clarín (Argentina), *El Observador* (Uruguay), *L'Osservatore Romano* (Vatican City), Religión Digital (Spain), and other websites specializing in religious information.

Twitter: @pontifex